24.95

"*Stan Chung is a beautiful writer who manages to balance strength and vulnerability with grace.*"

Kelly Doyle, PhD, English Instructor,
Kwantlen Polytechnic University

"*Compelling, highly personal, and from the heart. You'll feel Stan's pain, his joy and you'll root for him in his struggles.*"

Jon Manchester, News Editor of Castanet
former Managing Editor of the Kelowna Daily Courier

"*The best thing about Stan Chung's writing is that it's deeply real. Not to say his words and sentences are anything but beautiful; they are gorgeous. But he tears down pretence to reveal a simple honest truth in which we can see just a little bit of ourselves.*"

Naheen Nenshi
Mayor of Calgary, AB

"*In this collection, Stan Chung offers readers glimpses into his life as a father, son, husband, and citizen. These stories, like all personal writing, should act as mirrors as well as windows. In pondering his own hopes, confusions, and contradictions with frankness, humour, and tenderness, the author gently urges us to contemplate our own blessings and burdens, our own need to understand what we are and what we want to be.*"

Kelly Pitman,
English Department, Camosun College

Books by Stan Chung
Global Citizen: River of Love and Other Essays
I Held My Breath for a Year

STAN CHUNG

I Held My Breath for a Year

and other essays

Library and Archives Canada Cataloguing in Publication

Chung, Stan, author

    I held my breath for a year / Stan Chung.

This book celebrates ten years of the Global Citizen, a bi-weekly

    column published in the Okanagan Sunday.

Issued in print and electronic formats.

ISBN 978-1-987982-19-0 (paperback). — ISBN 978-1-987982-20-6

(html)

    I. Title.

PS8605.H85I44 2016   C814'.6   C2016-905790-9

                                     C2016-905791-7

Publication Assistance in Canada by:
Artistic Warrior Publishing
www.artisticwarrior.com

I dedicate this book to Alberta Susan Kamstra.
You are the love of my life.

Contents

Forward
by Jim Taylor

For about ten years, Stan Chung and I have written facing columns in the Okanagan Sunday newspaper; a joint publication of the Kelowna Courier and the Penticton Herald. My column, usually on the left hand Opinion page, usually dealt with social and justice issues in the news. Stan's, on the right hand page, explored the emotions that make humans tick.

I often wished I had the courage to write the way he does. Because Stan writes with an unflinching honesty. It's an almost ruthless refusal to sugar-coat the human condition. Whether it's about growing up as the only Asian kid in a small town, about mental illness, about family relationships or, for that matter, about educational philosophy, Stan is not content with superficial answers. He is almost forensic in his willingness to probe the attitudes and emotions that mould our behaviour. I hope he never writes about me!

Most of us – and I include myself – tend to sandpaper smooth the raw edges of our psyches. We find a rationalization to justify our actions. We manage to shift part of the blame to someone else. We kid ourselves that it will all work out all right, in the end.

We are amazingly good at self-deception. Stan refuses to buy into self-deception. He has an artist's eye for detail. He remembers the tree branch scratching at the window, the wind whispering around the eaves, the tear hovering at the edge of an eye. He remembers

1

the fear of being different, the foul taste of being bullied, the empty hole of being alone. I try to forget those things. But Stan exhumes them, rotates them, and learns his lessons from them.

Because Stan is an educator. He recognizes that all education has to start with personal experience. Anything else is just book-larnin' -- in one ear and out the other. In the classroom, he works with his students' experience. On the printed page, he works with his own experience, which is always, to some extent, also our experience. We read, we are moved, we understand ourselves better.

I carry a copy of Stan's first book, *Global Citizen*, with me in my car. When I have to sit and wait, perhaps while the cops sort out an accident on the highway, or while I wait for a granddaughter to emerge from the shopping mall, I pull that book out and read another chapter or two. I've read the whole thing at least twice. Yet I never fail to find at least one insight, one incident that reaches deep inside me and grabs my heart or my guts.

May it be so too for this book.

I Held My Breath For a Year

When I was a boy, someone used to leave messages for me on the trail to school. They were handwritten on white 8 x 11" paper. The messages lasted about a year. They started in Grade 8 and ended in Grade 9 when we moved away. They appeared mostly on Mondays.

Sometimes the paper was held down by rocks so the message wouldn't blow away. Sometimes the paper was taped to a skinny fir.

When I walked through the trees on my way to school, I always held my breath. Sometimes I would avoid the trail. Sometimes I would run as fast as I could.

Mostly, I kicked dirt over the paper and later, when I grew up, I just tried not to remember.

I have never told anyone what was written to me. The words were "Eff Off, Chinaman" or "No Chinks Allowed" or "I Will Kill You, Yellow Nigger."

It's difficult to remember exactly how I felt back then. I was always afraid. I felt in ways that I don't have the words to describe, despite the fact that I am a writer.

I can tell you now a fragment of my truth. I wanted to disappear. I felt helpless, like nothing.

To be frank, this was nothing compared to what other kids faced. Reserve girls were raped. Some kids went to school in the same shirt for a week. And we got used to kids who were just plain hungry. The new girl from India – well, I can't even describe the blank face of a child who has been terrorized.

In Canada today, we have come a long way from Williams Lake in the 1970s. We passed anti-hate and discrimination laws, and we do our best to be an inclusive society. We are a fair people. And unlike most other countries, we know equality of opportunity, not simplistic equality, is the answer.

So, I can't help but want to ask the child in me about what I endured. I also want to know how my early life shaped the adult that I have become.

For the most part, I turned out fine. I went to school, did what I was told and I have always been surrounded by loving family and friends.

So why is it that once in a while, someone says something at work or someone posts something on Facebook and I feel like that boy again, the boy who held his breath for a year?

There is no overt racism in my sphere anymore, but there are still the events sociologists call micro-aggressions.

Micro-aggressions are small acts committed by people with privilege that make us feel unwanted, hated or merely less than human.

Discrimination is systemic; its impact persists across generations and when you feel it, it can trigger you. My buttons get pushed and I become that boy again, holding my breath for a year.

I have learned strategies to deal with these micro-aggressions because it has been my usual response to do what I did as a boy. I did nothing. I said nothing. We are experts at doing nothing, not because we don't want to act, but often because we don't know how.

Today, I practice a strategy that begins with not accepting silence. Silence means agreement. It means acquiescing. I say to myself that to stand up for that boy within I can no longer accept silence.

So what does one say?

First of all, I repeat back the distressing words in a calm and dispassionate way. This distancing effect helps me calm my emotions and manage my anger.

I must admit that in the past I have over-reacted and this is wrong. Plus, it never works to shame anyone, no matter what.

So after I repeat the words, I state how I feel about them. It is important to own one's feelings as a way of being a witness to your own heart. I use the word witness very deliberately because being a self-witness is an effective way to be an ally to the child within, to humanity itself.

Self-witnessing is about actively resisting hurtful or ignorant words. It's also a way to monitor yourself and stand up for others. After I state my feelings, I invite a productive conversation about how to end the expression of thoughts and language that marginalize and hurt others.

I am not that great at self-witnessing, but it does work. It is a lot better than swearing at your steering wheel or kicking the cat. I believe self-witnessing is one important human competency. When we learn to stand up for ourselves, then we learn how to stand up for others. If we get good at standing up for the vulnerable and the unwanted, then we can call ourselves leaders.

When I think back to the person who left me those messages I wonder. But my main thought now is how to end hopelessness in our Indigenous youth.

We are a good people. When we hear bad things, it is an ethical act to stand up, especially if it is for those who cannot stand up for themselves. A more inclusive, more fair, and a more equitable place is what makes our country distinct and that is what makes me most proud of being a Canadian.

But we can do better.

Do Not Fly Away

His body was found hanging in a basement utility closet. I talked with him the night before. His voice sounded bright and sincere, as it usually did. He told me everything would be okay, that he was set, that plans had been made.

"Hey man," he'd said. "What's up? Everything is fine here," he'd said. "Just wanted to… just wanted to say…" Then his voice cracked. "Thank you."

"Thank me? For what?" I said.

"For, you know, being a good teacher to me."

My eyes filled up then, as they always do when I think of these words, and I wanted to hold him tight. Hold him tight so he would not fly away.

But we were on the telephone. So I did not much of anything. "Well," I said with forced cheer. "I'll talk to you later."

I needed to escape his gratitude. (I still keep the letter he wrote me in a desk drawer, and I have only read it once.) He was too much for me, this big kid.

Why was I always so afraid that he was going to say something sincere to me?

"Just a second," he said. There was a pause in the line. I thought I could hear him answering the door. Pizza delivery? I could hear traffic in the distance. His apartment was near Broadway. Maybe it was raining, too. Was that the sound of an electric trolley bus, the wires sparking and twitching overhead?

A few months before he called, we met in Prince George for the last time. It was spring, but still felt like winter. The last bit of grey snow remained in the ditches.

He took the bus up to see his mother. She was having a tough time. He'd lost his younger brother the year before in a car accident. His mother was now living alone in a single wide trailer in College Heights.

He told me about sitting with her. She talked endlessly about his younger brother while wiping tears with one hand and holding a cigarette and a glass of sherry in another.

"She's creating mythology," he said.

"Is she going to hold up?" I asked while we walked the grounds of the college where I worked.

"She feels stunned and blown away," he said. "Dad is right out of it too, but he's busy paying for what's-her-face's manicures and daycare."

"Wow," I said. "Can things unravel anymore?"

"It's like my brother was all that was holding us together," he said. "My older brother won't talk to me. My mother is a mess. And Dad has a new family now. He's dying his hair. He's driving truck. We're like oil on water now. Dispersing."

"I'm sorry," I said.

It was a blue-sky day. A distant blue like you only see in the north. The cars and logging trucks roared along the bypass that cut through the middle of town. He wore corduroys and brown suede shoes with crepe soles. I grabbed his arm and steered him away from some dog droppings.

"May in Prince George is fragrant," he said. "Pulp mill

combined with thawing dog crap."

"Yeah," I said. "It's spring."

"You don't have to worry about me."

"I've known you since you were 19," I said. "What are you, 26 now?"

"I have to tell you something," he said and stopped. I listened to him tell me about a series of appointments he had had with a psychiatrist.

"How does the medication make you feel?"

"I don't know. Like tasting through gauze. Like being underwater. All the usual pharmacological clichés."

"Can you stand it?"

"I don't know."

"What does the doctor say?"

"He says I might be medicated for the rest of my life. Let me put it this way: It's not getting any better. I have a psychological illness. I can't hold a thought."

"That's terrible."

I looked at him. He was tall and handsome, his smile broad and genuine. People loved him. He could talk with anybody.

"I should get going," I said. I knew that I should have said something more, done something different than what I actually did which was just to stand there and look up the Nechako river cut banks and the spirals of white smoke coming up from the pulp mill.

"You know much about pain?" he asked suddenly.

What I know about pain isn't very insightful.

"Sometimes I hear voices," he said.

"What do they say?"

"They say that when you're in pain you wonder if you can stand another minute."

***

I can barely remember his roommate who told me that they had found his body.

She was new, somebody who didn't know him well. She called and told me, and I didn't know what to do with the information.

"He talked about you," she said.

"I'm just a teacher of his," I said. "I talked with him the night before."

"He said nice things about you," she said.

***

There was no funeral to attend. No memorial service. At the time, I didn't know how common this was. We just don't know how to handle suicide. We are at once sad, guilty and ashamed.

I wanted to call his friends and let them know, but since I was only a teacher, I didn't really know his current circle.

I wanted to do a lot of things. In short, I did nothing.

When I think about this boy, this tall beautiful boy, I think about his journey. He was the first in his family to go to university. He was the first in his family to prefer deconstructing poetry to slapping a puck. He put his sensitivities to use at university. He showed me A+ essays he had received in both Sociology and English. He talked about a future as a lawyer. He talked about making his mother proud.

I thought I sat on the outskirts of his life, but I realize now that I was wrong. I was his teacher, and teachers can play a central role, even if the contact is infrequent. But this is not a story about teachers.

There is a story to every suicide. For many, his loss is a riddle to be solved, even if for me the answer to the riddle is quite mundane. But his life is not a detective story. This is not a story about why.

In the letter that he wrote me, the letter that I have had the courage to read only once, he told me that, "We all have a reckless disregard for love."

His mother loved him, but could only talk about his lost brother. His older brother loved him, but could not understand his pain. His father loved him, but only at a safe distance.

There is no one to blame. We have all lost people. We still feel their absence. I miss him, even though he has been gone for many years.

I don't care so much about the details of what happened because I care more about who he was. I care about what he could have been. I care about what he meant to me.

In the corridors and corners of my heart, he walks with me just as he did that spring afternoon in Prince George. I hear his footsteps beside mine. I hear him laugh and smile.

I am gone away, he says. But you are a part of me.

I whisper his name in the mornings between sleep and walking. I love you. You honoured me by calling me teacher.

And I don't blame myself anymore for you being gone.

***

If you're having suicidal thoughts,
please call the Crisis Line in your community.

Idiot's Guide to Busting Stress

Stress takes its toll on my body. My neck really aches. You too? My lower back is on the fritz. You too? If it's Wednesday, it must be a migraine. Thursday? Probably a bad digestion day.

Like Wi-Fi, sometimes stress feels like it is beaming in from everywhere. We love our jobs – we hate the stress. We love our families – we hate the fighting. Let's tell the truth: stress is the source of nearly every illness. Mastering it may be the source of wisdom.

When we discuss the solutions to the problem of stress, certain words keep coming up. Balance. Exercise. Meditation. Yoga. Spirit. Letting go.

Stress is killing us. What do we do? I only know the things that work for me. And the only thing that really works takes a lot of practice.

It's called detachment. Detachment is not easy. When you do it well, you can compartmentalize your stress, manage it and even find ways to set it free. Detachment is a tricky practice. Whether you're trying to achieve a championship putt or trying to put your crying child to bed, detachment can help us manage our stress.

These are the five basic practices of detachment.

Detachment of Time

We live in the here and now, but our stress comes from being helplessly stuck in the past or the future. You hear the voices of your childhood tormentors. Or you can't stop stressing about your next meeting, deadline or challenge. To practise detachment from the past and the future, pay attention to now. The best way to do this is to listen to yourself breathing. Breathing is the body's reminder of the eternal moment. Conscious breathing brings with it incredible stress release. It's why swimming, jogging, and meditation can be so healing.

Detachment of Responsibility

We think we are responsible for everything. We are not. We can only do so much. One person can certainly make a difference, but martyrdom is not the answer. Sometimes, it feels like no matter what we do, it is never enough and we blame ourselves. Detachment can also come in the form of trust. Trust others to do their part. Trust the sun to come up tomorrow. Trust others to make mistakes. (They will fix them, too, not you.) Trust in the Universe. This is the art of letting go. Practice letting go of your sense of responsibility by putting your faith in a positive universe.

Detachment of Consequence

We care so much about the outcome, the winning or the losing, that the stress burns up our insides. Victory and defeat can be the same thing. Success and failure are only temporary conditions. The win/lose paradigm is a sure-fire way to stress ourselves out. Instead of stressing about outcomes, focus your energies instead on performance. Focus on performing through informed practice. Get a coach to help you practise those essential skills. If you practise and perform well, the consequences will take care of themselves.

Detachment of Desire

Attachment causes suffering. The more you want, the more

disappointed you can be. What if you tried not wanting? What if you tried seeing that desire is almost always a function of peer or social pressure? We are social animals: it is natural to want what others want. But what happens if you practise not wanting what others want? You begin to come free. Start with small things. Do things your own way. Worry less about appearance. To master our desires is to master ourselves. The first step in mastering ourselves is to detach ourselves from the desires of others.

Detachment of Self

Much of our stress is ego-related. Our egos are pretty darn sensitive. We desire to be loved. When someone says something critical, we cannot separate the criticism from the person who criticized us. Our egos tell us we must win. We must be successful. Our egos tell us we must own the right things at the right age. The detachment of self is a huge stress buster. Self-mastery comes through the practice of humility. Detachment teaches us to see the ego, to understand its suffering, and to choose whether to obey its cries.

The five practices of detachment tell us to be attentive to all situations. The attached person can sometimes be swayed and easily manipulated by emotions. The detached person knows that all arguments and positions deserve respect.

Even difficult business and family decisions become easier if we find detachment. Do the research; search out the facts. We know that we are highly emotional creatures. By attempting to practise detachment, we experience our emotions as only one perspective.

We are so much more than individual examples of a species. Detachment may reveal our connection to each other and to our spiritual natures.

The collective stress of our planet seen from the moon looks a lot different than the puny individual stress of a traffic tantrum. We are not alone in our stress. We are not alone in our caring too much, being too self-absorbed and being too worried about what others think.

When viewed from the distance of the moon, stress changes its intensity. Instead of seeing ourselves as helplessly locked in a complex world of impossible demands, detachment allows us to see our own humanity.

Like you, I have a lot of stress right now. I worry about the planet, the state of our communities. I worry about my job, my kids, my mortgage, and trying to be good. That is why I practise the five detachments. So I can find balance in my life. So I can see myself and others compassionately, forgive myself and others for not doing more, and make the absolute most of right now.

Last Day
with Father

Today's the day I see my father for the last time. Flat low building in Burnaby. Sky. Trees moving in the distance. Choking in my throat.

"I don't know what he'll be like," I say.

"Are you alright?" says my wife. "It's only been 16 years."

Time to see him one last time. Time to see him alive. So that I can write this.

Look for reception. The light seems different here. Families meeting with patients. Room 26.

A man walks down the hall toward me. Hair still wet. Slim. Youthful. Hardly any gray for a man in his 70s. Well-looked after you'd say.

Not frightening. Not violent. Not anymore. For a moment I become a small little boy.

Mental illness, my sister says, works like a preservative on the body. He doesn't look like a dying man.

The stomach cancer is closing off the top of his stomach. His organs are failing. He looks stranded here in a hospice of dying people. He looks more alive than all of us.

"Hello, Dad," I hear myself say.

He's wearing plastic slippers. Something for the beach. He points to a chair. He sits on the bed. He looks thin. Black eyes. Bright. Alert.

"Who are you?"

"I'm Stan."

"Stan?"

"Your son. Stan and Heidi. Your children."

"Stan and Heidi." He nods. A memory firing.

"You have children?" he asks.

"Yes. Two."

"How old?"

"Seven and nine. A boy and a girl."

"You live in Prince George?"

"Kelowna now."

"Yes. You came down."

"Yes. We came down," I say.

"Why?"

I freeze.

"To see you."

"Me. Why?" I don't know what to say and change tack.

"Hey, Dad. How are you doing? What are you doing these days?" I am so controlled.

"Not so good," he says. Points to his stomach. Closes his eyes. I realize he's holding himself together.

"My time is up," he says quietly.

"Are you in pain, Dad?"

"No, it's okay," he gestures with hands. He closes his eyes. He goes away for a little while. A breath.

"We're here on vacation, Dad. We're going to Campbell River. Remember Campbell River? You were a minister there. We used to camp at Miracle Beach. Do you remember? You picked oysters at Oyster Bay and ate them raw on the shore."

I laugh with my father after years of estrangement.

Light shifts. Clouds must be passing outside. I have a recognition now. No more fear. I move to the bed and sit beside him.

"I should get going now, Dad. If you don't mind. I'd like to visit you again."

"It's okay."

"You drove down?"

"Yeah, it's just four hours."

"Why?"

"You're my father."

He looks at me. I face his eyes. Black coals. I cannot bear it. I move my hand to cover his. Hold his hand. Tight.

"It's okay," I say.

He faces me. A sob comes from deep in his throat. He is crying now. I move closer. Hold both his hands. Closer again. Hold his body in my arms. His chest is hollow, like a bird. Ribs so light. So fragile.

"You were a good dad," I say. "You were a very good dad."

I say these words without thinking. No tears from me. Not yet. I will feel this all later, I think. Maybe a year later, I think. Maybe ten. In 2016.

My father walks me to the door. Plastic slippers on his feet. Courteous again. A different person somehow. I walk slowly. I cannot look at him. I cannot look back.

Trembling inside. Greet the outside air. See the sky. Hold this feeling before it disappears. Quickly now. Make up a face for my wife, son, and daughter. Lean against the van. Wonder. About him. About the colour of the sky.

He will die a few days later. Lie down and never rise again.

Today's a good day to die, he will tell the nurse. It is ten years later now. I am hiding in these words.

Incarceration of Father Part 1

At first she did nothing because that was her nature. My mother felt his hands upon her throat. He was yelling something at her. She could smell his stale breath. His eyes were narrowed and his jaw firm. Madness erupted in his eyes.

She had been dreaming. He shook her, and she struggled for air. She thought about death. She considered closing her eyes and allowing him murder. Why not give him his way?

He was her husband. She followed him dutifully. He had been the biggest influence in her life. They had been married in a small church in 1961, surrounded by security forces. They went to the sand beaches of Pusan for their honeymoon, swimming on the beach, posing on a rock for a photograph, making love again and again in their hotel room. She has given him two children, followed him to Canada, worked as a campus chambermaid, and lived dutifully as a minister's wife.

She twisted sideways. The room darkened. She looked through the Venetian blinds and glimpsed a corner of the blue sky. Fading, fading.

This is not my husband, she told herself and twisted her body sideways. This is mental illness. She gasped for air and rolled her knees upward. She thrust outward and pushed him backward. He fell off the bed. He banged his head against a bookshelf.

She dashed out of the room. She ran out of the apartment

coughing and crying. Her throat began to swell.

My mother met my father in Korea during the 60s when she came to military intelligence as a French translator.

It wasn't long before she entered a training program. They asked what kind of career she dreamed about. She told them broadcaster. And so they groomed her, trained her, and prepared her for a position in broadcasting. Few assets were more valuable than those that worked in the media.

That was what he told her before he decided to keep her as his own. No doubt she found his power and influence attractive. He was a charismatic, intense young man with a burning intellect and a disarming smile.

They shared some common values. He had been raised on Cheju under Japanese occupation. She had been raised under Japanese occupation in Manchuria. Among other things, they both enjoyed Japanese food. She loved fashion, dancing, dogs, and jewelry. He loved fishing, reading, swimming, and politics. When he went abroad he brought Chanel perfume. Throughout my childhood, I remember most the times my mother packed her bags and told us she had to get away. At five years old, I remember telling her not to leave us with him. At ten, I insisted she get a divorce. At fifteen, I practiced karate so that I would be ready to help her escape.

When I was a boy, I did not know the things that I know now. How could I know what kind of father I had? How could I know what he whispered to my mother to keep her from leaving?

I was her son. I grew knowing that there were things she wanted that my father could not give. But aside from small things I didn't know what she needed. She often told us how things would have been different if she had a career as a journalist.

"Then, you would have married another man and we wouldn't exist," I would say.

"I know," she would sigh. "I know."

They were my parents. I knew only them. I had no other comparisons. I did not know what kind of family I belonged to. I did not know what was normal. The pictures on our black and white television of families likes the Bunkers, the Waltons, the Bradys, only made me wonder more.

In retrospect, I realize all children feel this way. Our families are strange and wonderful. The people who feed us, raise us, and transfer their values to us are also connected to the past and to their own families.

Our ancestors become us. The line that connects us goes spiraling backward and we realize that connection cannot be broken, no matter how we try. No matter what we become.

So when I put my father into a mental institution, removed my mother from her home and moved her across town, I wondered if they had somehow prepared me to be my parent's caregiver. I never failed to live up to my duties as the first son.

I did my duty. I heeded my father's word. He told me take care of him if he ever got violent. I heeded my responsibility to my mother. We got her government job back through political contacts and old friends. We found her an apartment in Kitsilano near the beach. But the one thing I could not do was go the Burnaby Psychiatric Centre and see my father. In truth, I was afraid.

Even though I was a grown man, thirty-two years old, an English professor with a family of my own, I became a helpless child in the company of my 5'5", 130 pound father. It was more than just the schizophrenia.

My love for him had manifested itself in two ways: firstly, in acts of mutiny and revolt; secondly, in desperate acts of a son seeking his father's approval.

I have spent a good deal of my life reaching to my father. I desperately wanted his endorsement, his admiration. He is connected to me in ways that I do not understand. He is my sail and my anchor. He is my father and my tormentor, my inspiration and my foe. He had been a deadly soldier, a political revolutionary, and charismatic preacher. But to me, he was my dad.

As I thought these things one blustery day in 1992, the telephone rang. It was a male nurse from the psychiatric ward. My father had demanded to know who was responsible for his incarceration. The nurses were shocked by his command, his vocabulary, and his forcefulness.

When one of the nurses tried to give him a sedative, my father moved decisively. He quickly overwhelmed three male nurses, breaking a nose, and removing an elbow from its proper position, and escaped.

The RCMP had been notified. They asked me where he might go. I told me that I didn't know.

I knew he was coming for me.

Incarceration of Father Part II

In August of 1992, two RCMP officers came to the door of my parent's condo and told me the news. My father had escaped. He had overpowered three male nurses and somehow slipped out of the locked mental facility in Burnaby. One of the nurses had a dislocated arm, the other a busted nose.

"Does your father have martial arts training?" the tall officer asked.

"A black belt," I mumbled. My father taught karate every Thursday night when I was a teenager in Williams Lake.

"It says here that he's a retired minister."

"Yup," I said. I didn't tell them that in addition to commando training, he ran the Korean CIA in the early 60s; a force with thousands of employees including the French translator he would marry, my mother. I also left out the part about him wearing a concealed handgun in Seoul and sleeping with it under the pillow.

"Do you have any idea where your father might be? He's got no money or identification."

"And, he's got no shoes," said the tall officer.

"I don't know where he could be," I said looking out at the Coast Mountains. The afternoon sky was like concrete. I felt a sick feeling coming over me. I was thirty years old. My father was a slender, shy senior who weighed maybe 130 pounds.

And I was still afraid of him.

* * *

A few months before my father's big escape he and my mother visited me in Prince George where I taught college English.

It was the last weekend in May, a brief moment that we northerners call spring. The apple tree in my front yard sported little white flowers. They parked their '86 Toyota van out in front. The Mercedes had been long sold.

"Why are you sleeping in the van, Dad? I've got a perfectly acceptable bed you can use. I'll sleep in the basement. It's no trouble."

"I prefer it for safety reasons," he said.

"Is that why you're lining your fishing hat with tin foil?" I said.

"Don't you question me!" he shouted and walked out.

* * *

Mental illness is fairly challenging for any family, to put it mildly. If you listen to the doctors, you learn to separate the illness from the person.

It was the illness that caused my father to try to choke the life out of my mother. It was the illness that made him believe he could pick lottery numbers, thereby forcing my mother to quit her government job. It was the illness that caused him to point out the invisible creatures sitting on people's shoulders.

"Want me to drown the little flabby devil on your shoulder?" he would ask.

"What's the little guy doing?" I would ask.

"He's staring at his friends around your feet."

What made my father's illness particularly problematic was the 50/50 principle: half of what my dad said was utterly ridiculous. For example, he worried that mom was poisoning his food. He worried that North Korean soldiers were invading the condo. I thought I was cool with the crazy stuff. But what really got me was the other 50 per cent. The stuff that was half true.

He suggested to my sister that a certain old family friend was a pedophile. My sister, when she heard this, refused to talk about it, other than saying that yes, this was probably true. I think it was true.

My father was obsessed with sexuality, religion, and literary figures. He talked about people's auras. He talked about the spirit world. He spoke to the dead. He talked as if he was tapped into the timeless unseen world in a way that made my skin crawl. At times, I desperately wanted to talk to someone, but nobody wants to talk about mental illness.

On one visit, I couldn't stand the half-truths anymore, so I called the local paranormal society.

"My father says he sees ghosts and spirits. You wouldn't happen to know any people who can verify this kind of stuff?"

"Sure, we'll be right over." I imagined the van from the film *Ghostbusters* pulling up to the house, but instead a man and two women arrived together in a rather tired Ford Tempo. If you had access to unseen power and vision, wouldn't you make a better choice of automobile?

I dragged him out of the Toyota, so I could put him on display. They said hello to him. One of the women acted like a medium because she closed her eyes a lot and fingered the white crystals around her neck. The younger of the women had long black hair with a tie-dyed bandana around it. The man wore a trimmed beard, wire framed glasses, and carried himself as if he were the leader. Actually, he looked more like a guy who might be good at fixing computers.

My father answered a few questions and said. "I'm going to leave now. Please accept your homosexuality, sir. And I can smell the illness in you women. Go see a doctor. You have internal problems." The three sat silently and listened to the door slam.

"Your father's aura is black," said the woman with the tie-dyed bandana.

"What does that mean?" I said. The man spoke slowly, rubbing his eyes.

"It means that he's very difficult to read. Your father's very troubled. I'm not getting a good feeling."

"And his power is rather… daunting,"

"Really," I said. "What should I do?"

"There is nothing we can do to help. Just think about the white light."

"What about his self-hypnosis?" I said. "What about his conversations with General Douglas MacArthur? What about all that stuff he said about your homosexuality, sir?"

"Fill yourself with white light. We have to leave," said the man. So that was that. My father scared off the paranormals. Everybody was scared. I was scared. My mother was scared. My family doctor was scared. The cops were scared.

* * *

I rented a science fiction movie and asked my friend Wing Sui to come over. I told him I was scared. "You don't talk like that," he said, and came over. I told him in self-pity, my father was on the loose, and he held me responsible.

At around 8 p.m. there was a knock on the door. I looked in the peep hole with my heart racing. It was the police officers, Laurel and Hardy. My father had been spotted. He had spent the day on the eighth floor visiting with some retired folks. He was gone again, this time with shoes and money. He had been in the building the whole time.

Later that night I tried to close my eyes. I could hear the jumbled, chaotic sounds of the city. I could not sleep. I was waiting to hear him calling my name from below, my Korean name, the name he used when I was a boy.

When I came to Canada, I cried at night a lot. He always sat on the edge of my bed touching my forehead.

I heard sirens. The traffic lights reflected on the ceiling. It was hot, so I opened the windows and blinds. Someone in the condo above watched a religious channel. A man was preaching.

In Prince George those few nights my parents visited, I could not sleep either. I slept downstairs. For the first time in my life, I faced a kind of fear that I can only call supernatural. My mind was jagged in ways I cannot describe.

Before I rented the house, someone killed themselves in it. In the darkness, I thought I heard voices and felt myself on the verge of disappearing. What must it have been like to lose your mind? Oh, the fear.

I could not stop my fear until I filled myself with a simple realization: it was the disease talking, not him. It was the disease talking, not my father. It was my guilt, fear and sorrow talking, not my own version of his disease.

The next day I saw him.

Incarceration of Father Part III

"Hi, Dad," I said. He was stretched out on a narrow cot. He opened his eyes and stared up at the ceiling without blinking. My father wore a faded golf shirt, khakis, and jogging shoes. His hands were folded over his chest as if he were in a coffin.

The lights were off. A narrow window provided a faint glow. The traffic sounds were muted. A woman wearing headphones operated a gas-powered trimmer along the edge of the building. Rat, tat, tat, tat.

Go right in, said the nurse, a tall man with a clipboard and a beard. Your dad's been getting some shut eye. He had a hint of a tattoo, barbed wire peeking out of his short-sleeved shirt.

The nurse smiled and moved a chair. A few minutes earlier we had chatted about my father's background.

"Yeah, man," he had said. "Your old man's like a priest-slash-warrior, a soldier, founding father of Korea, a United Church minister."

"Yeah, he set the bar," I had said.

The psychiatric centre on Willingdon Avenue in Burnaby had two sets of locked doors. There was plenty of visitor parking even though there were at least thirty beds. You could see why nobody wanted to visit the place. The wind had pushed a pile of orange leaves against the single door entrance. The place looked abandoned.

I wanted to skulk away and go back to my hotel. Instead, I

grabbed the door and opened it.

In the 1990s the BC government closed a place called Riverview Hospital in Coquitlam. It was an infamous institution, a place where you put people away. Apparently, they put a lot of people on the street when they closed. They were to be reabsorbed by their communities.

Now, I imagined, everyone was on the loose. They were under overpasses, in rooming houses, on couches, and in emergency rooms. When the police found my father, they handcuffed him and took him to Burnaby General where he sat in a rubber room without any furniture for 12 hours. They thought he would harm himself.

How did this all happen?

I looked at my father. His eyes were empty. He was thoroughly medicated. He blinked slowly like he was slowing down time. I sat down on the chair beside the bed.

"Who are you?" he asked.

"I'm just checking up on you," I said.

"I don't know who you are!"

"I'm your son," I said. "You have a son and daughter. Stan and Heidi. You named us. We are your family."

"Get out! You're not my family."

"Hey. I am your son," I said. He looked away. I watched him blink. "Dad, I put you here."

"What?" he stared at me.

"I put you here," I said slowly.

"You? Why?"

"Because you told me to. Because you said that it was my job to look after you and Mom. Because I'm your son."

"You are nothing." My father's shoulders slumped.

"Okay," I said. "I am nothing." His eyes softened. I moved to the bed and put my hand on his shoulder. His shoulders were bony. The rat-tat-tat from the trimmer stopped.

He began to sob then, shoulders shaking, nose running.

"Are you okay, Dad?"

"Why did you say I wasn't a good daddy?" he said, recalling a telephone conversation I had with him a few months before. After his spring visit to Prince George, he called and wanted to know why I had not visited him more.

Why? He had asked. So I told him in words I had never used before.

I said, Because. Because you were not a good father to me. It was the voice of the child, his child, the one who was still angry. He hung up right away. I phoned back. He sobbed and then he hung up again.

And now, in the middle of a psychiatric holding cell, my father wanted to know if I really meant what I had said . . . "you were not a good father to me."

"Why did you say that?" he asked. I looked at my father. The skin around his eyelids sagged. I thought of how many Sundays I stood at the front of the church after the service was over, waiting, like all the others, to shake his hand. How he would look right through me and then past me to the others.

"Dad," I said carefully. "I have been a bad son. You have been a good father. You made me strong. You listen to me now, okay? You listen to me." Tears flowed from my eyes and I choked out some more words. "I am sorry. I didn't take care of you properly. I should have."

* * *

On my father's neck there was a scar, a small white line. I once asked my father, on one of those terrible nights when I used to cry, where he got the scar.

"How did you get it, Daddy?"

"It's from a bullet. Now go to sleep."

"From a gun?"

"Yes," he said. "You used to play with my combat helmet when you were small. The helmet had many marks from bullets."

"What did you want to be when you were a boy, Dad? When you were eight years old?"

"I wanted to be president of my country," he said. "I lived under Japanese occupation on Cheju Island. I dreamed of an independent Korea."

"Daddy?"

"Yes, Son?"

"What will I be? What will I be? Will I fight in wars? Will I start a coup?"

"You, my son, you will be a man of principle."

"I will."

Whenever I recall that conversation, I feel my father to be larger than life, a man of great wisdom and purpose. A man who began a country, ministered to hundreds, and raised two children. He was the man I had wanted so much to impress. He was the man I would ultimately disappoint.

* * *

When I was 30 years old, my father became very ill. He hurt my mother and I had to take action. I signed the paperwork and made sure he received treatment, even though it was against his will, even though I would lose him.

I have accepted my role in his life.

I tried to take care of him but I couldn't. I was not able to overcome my feelings. For the next decade, my sister, who is generous and dispassionate, took care of his affairs. I listened to my sister who would tell me how much the social workers and nurses enjoyed him.

I have not met any of these people.

And then on a fall morning a few years ago, my father announced to the hospice nursing staff that it was a good day to die.

I think he had been waiting a long time to be able to say something like that.

He is reported to have spoken the words with energy and precision even though his stomach cancer was causing him great pain. Of course, he refused painkillers, preferring to meditate.

Then my father walked to his room at the end of the hall, put away his meagre belongings, took off his shoes, folded his hands across his chest, and closed his eyes.

The Three

Secrets of Failure

In 1966, Leonard Cohen wrote an experimental novel called *Beautiful Losers*. I've always liked the book, especially the title. When we misunderstand people, we like to call them losers. But when you look seriously, you realize that winning and losing are much more connected than we might think.

In order to win, we must lose. Ask any coach, teacher or billionaire. The victory of success depends on the art of failure. However, we don't respect the idea of failure in our culture. We gloss over failure, we demonize it, and we like to put it behind us. But, failure is the secret to success.

The scholarly research into expertise development has a special phrase for what we might commonly call failure: informed practice. Instead of seeing failure as the final step or outcome, experts tell us to see failure as part of a continuum of informed practice.

Entrepreneurs who have successfully sold their companies, do not achieve these astronomical paydays on their first try. They know that failure is just one step. Successful people conceive failure differently.

How do you respond to failure?

Seeing failure as an informed practice is at the heart of many world champions in sport. When you are beaten by someone who is faster, stronger, or more skilled some athletes quit; others train harder. Still others work hard at understanding how they define success and failure. It is productive to examine failure from three perspectives.

Secret 1 - Fail Fast

Failing fast means that you don't spend ten years working on perfecting something. In product testing, it is a lot smarter to create a rapid prototype and test it with an audience. It is not wise to work on something in secret for many years on the fantasy that you are developing something special. Never bank on just one idea. Instead, bank on the person who develops the ideas.

What is the difference between an entrepreneur/artist/scientist/builder and someone who is on the verge of bankruptcy? The entrepreneur knows that it may take seven business concept experiments to find the right one. The bankrupt person depends on one concept and has no real contingency plans. Failing fast means developing and testing your ideas quickly and moving on.

Secret 2 - Fail Cheap

Failing cheap means not wasting hard earned cash or invaluable energy on untested ideas. Becoming emotionally tied to a project will help you burn through a lot of resources before you wake up and realize that it is time to move on. Over-investing in one idea is akin to betting all your money on one race horse. Diversify your projects, spread out your risk, and be loyal to an honest assessment of what works with a diverse audience.

Failing cheap will allow you to invest in your own capabilities rather than investing in a business model that might easily be duplicated.

Secret 3 - Fail Beautifully

Failing beautifully means changing your mindset about failure.

It's time to stop beating yourself up with language that is not productive. People will respect honesty, but there is a point where you have to stop calling yourself a loser. Stop believing that quitting something is wrong.

Quitting something that is not working for you is often the very wisest thing you can do. Life is short. Be positive. Love yourself and get used to the idea that there will be a few bumps on the road of life. Change gears, rev up, and move forward. Successful people learn from their mistakes. Let go of your failures by thinking about them as valuable learning experiments.

Failing beautifully means seeing failure differently. Deciding that it is time to move on is a sign of maturity. Not allowing failure to impact your self-esteem is the mark of a resilient human being.

Another way of changing your mind about failure is seeing your projects as learning experiments. A mindset that is constantly experimenting with new ideas is the hallmark of a culture of innovation.

Do you expect innovation? Innovation experts say that reconceiving failure is the key.

In our education system, we do not understand the importance of failing beautifully. Children get labelled very early with failure. This takes a terrible toll. Learning to fail in a culture of innovation where it is important and acceptable requires us all to reconceive what failure truly means.

Learning and failure go hand in hand. A deep knowledge of learning tells us that failure is a vital part of knowledge. We should be kind to ourselves when we fail.

We should respect those who have the courage to fail in our society. Are you an artist, entrepreneur, scientist, teacher? Let us build a community where we can all learn to fail fast, fail cheap, and fail beautifully.

Who wants to fail? Who wants to undergo the social judgement? We should all embrace failure and those out there making a go of it. Don't listen to those people who have never been out there with their face in the wind of criticism. If it is worth it, you will be knocked down.

I am a failure in many things. I am working on many things. I am constantly experimenting. Sometimes I think I cannot take any more, but in the same moment, I know that failure is one of the most beautiful aspects of life.

Leonard Cohen is right; losers are beautiful. A beautiful person is one who loves you and accepts you.

Refuge into Nothing: The Mysterious Language of Stillness

These words are about nothing. Nothing is an advanced word. It is more than a word for yoga masters, philosophers, and artists: nothing is everything.

First, there is stillness. There is nothing moving after . . . after all is said and done. When there is stillness, the world is as motionless as a snow covered crocus petal.

Finding stillness may be more elusive than unearthing gold or diamonds. In fact, the more we own, the more we may be owned by the sad frenzy of ownership. Nothing is a different kind of wealth. It is an empty stage after a performance. Satisfied and quiet.

Nothing is the stillness in your heart after gardening, after lovemaking. After the candle of your life has been extinguished by the wind.

After the ceremony of burial, your particular nothing is fragrant smoke across the open sky of your ancestors.

Nothing is also the past. It is the stillness before . . . before the April spring, before the ache of prayer. Before the moment before the moment.

How still is your moment? How still?

Before the beginning, before action. Before the stage lights shine down on the performance of your life.

Nothing is this space right now. The nowness of this exquisite moment with you and these words, your hot tea, the silver light in your eyes. The sound between my heartbeat and yours.

The infinite possibly of sensing our connected disconnectedness. You are with me?

Stillness is more than a challenge for us. My life often feels ablaze. The cacophony of fear and mistrust does more than disturb the peace.

The global polyphony calls forth how unfinished we are, how immature, how burdened by the limits of knowledge and language.

Nothing is the land that contains the poetry of what we do not know. The land of nothing is so difficult to learn. The vocabulary is captured in the silhouette of branches against the sky. The moon is calling our waters for unspoken vowels.

The eye of the hunted animal is our grammar.

If only I could receive the nothing signal, open the bandwidth of my soul. Sense the wilderness of nothing. The pleasure of being without. Pure being, rooted in land – in stones and blood.

Nothing is not human. It is more than human.

Beyond the stillness, there is still more to be learned from nothing. There is clearing your mind. Oh, how difficult it is to get clear, find clear, feel clear, be clear.

Are you in the clear?

My mind is like blowing sand. I feel scattered. Unable to find the refuge of nothing, to map the clearing beyond the grains of our million worries. Why is it so difficult to clear the mind when I know my thoughts are merely for the selecting?

I select. I choose nothing but nothing.

What does nothing sound like? Yes, it sounds like listening. Deep listening is not about hearing, it is the sound of the Other, of our Connectedness.

The electricity of love. At first it sounds like nothing. Slow down and you can hear the sound of your listening.

Listening reverberates across all land and time. Listening is older than time. It is the sound of nothing, holding us, cherishing silence, finding stillness in our hammering hearts, finding love in the desolation.

Discovering sanctuary at the dark bottom of each moment.

The Morning Before Reconciliation

"Reconciliation is not an Aboriginal program; it is a
Canadian one. Virtually all aspects of Canadian society
may need to be reconsidered."
Truth and Reconciliation Commission Report 2015

My professor friend in Victoria, BC, has Irish ancestry and also
teaches Irish literature. Only recently did she announce her error
in calling Ireland a white country. She bravely admits that her
received Irishness is essentially a whitewashed version of a cultural
stereotype.

"I used to think the Irish in me made me whiter than white,"
she says, as we chat on Facebook.

"Really," I say. "Is there ever a point in Ireland's history where
there was just *one* version of being Irish?"

"Absolutely not," she says. "When the Irish came to North
America, they found themselves still subject to much harassment
and harm. They were banned from certain professions, certain
neighbourhoods, and even from white drinking establishments, for
example, in Boston. There was strong marginalization of the Irish
by the British who used nearly the same racialized language and
cultural condemnation as we see with Canadian First Nations."

"Now you have green beer, shamrocks, and leprechauns," I say.

"Exactly," she says. "Whiteness didn't begin as a cliché. On the contrary, the Irish needed to become *white* to be accepted. One way was to join in oppressing others with different skin colours. Another was to engage in self-imposed erasure of cultural history and repackage that history as stereotype. We still make Irish jokes that would be unacceptable for any other culture, right?"

"Maybe whiteness," I say, "is also a form of cultural hybridity. There are many shades of white that become subsumed by the forces of the dominant mass culture. When a Scot marries a German, from the outside it looks like one shade of white is produced, but clearly some rituals carry on, others are adapted, a new hybrid of say fried pickled cabbage and sausages is formed by the unification."

"That's almost funny," she says.

"Perhaps marriage produces the first hybridity," she says with a laugh. My Victoria friend will teach Irish literature in Ireland this spring. She wants to show the concept of how whiteness produces both hybridity *and* erasure in order to interrogate the forces that produce identity and belonging. So much for close reading and memorizing the verses of Yeats.

My parents, grandparents, and I have long been faced with a *one-faced notion* of what it means to be a so-called Asian. My Canadian friends used to ask me in jest what a Korean was and whether I could tell the difference between a Korean, Chinese, and Japanese. Look, they pointed, what is that guy? Did you know that some Canadian Indigenous peoples who have intermarried are lovingly called *Chindians*?

What exactly is an Asian or an Indian? Is it as meaningless or as complex a term as white?

A good example of the spiraling complexities is the comfort women in World War II. The Koreans are demanding compensation for Korean comfort women who were held by Japanese soldiers as sexual slaves during WWII. But the Vietnamese are also claiming to be victims of the same phenomenon with Korean soldiers as the perpetrators during the Vietnam War. Dutch comfort women who were captured in Indonesia were also comfort women of the Japanese with captured Korean soldiers manning the gates.

Can it get more complex?

Yes, it can. The inclusion of the United States using atomic bombs to kill at least 129,000 in Nagasaki and Hiroshima also brings this war-time confluence of racialized trauma into sharp relief. The cycle of victims and the legacy of trauma for all agents and victims of war seems a part of the human struggle we call colonization.

I don't know how, but I truly feel the generational trauma of countless decades of colonization. I felt it in my parents and grandparents. I feel it in the work I do with Indigenous peoples as not only an urgent call, but also a space of sharp anger and enduring patience.

Will we overcome our traumas?

Immigrants and newcomers may be able to use their own histories to recognize the losses and gains and ambivalences of colonization, but we may never understand the generational trauma the Indigenous peoples of Canada have endured.

The CBC has suspended commentary on its online news stories featuring Indigenous themes. The commentary is so incendiary that the CBC does not feel it can successfully moderate. One of the common questions asked by settlers was "Why don't you people just get over it?" Another common question is "I'm not personally responsible in any way for the harms you've suffered, so why should I feel guilty?"

These questions, and others like them, point to the difficulty of achieving reconciliation in all walks of Canadian life. Reconciliation itself is a contested notion, so some point to divisions within the Indigenous community as justifications for not participating.

What is not so clear is what Indigenous people and settlers have in common when it comes to surviving and living with the impact of colonization.

Trauma as it has existed through institutional racism, extermination through law, and many other official and unofficial manifestations of Canada's system of apartheid, will require much more than a focus on Indigenous healing.

As the TRC suggests, this is Canada's issue.

The TRC and other organizations, including the United Nations, call for immediate changes to the living conditions and human rights of Indigenous peoples, but they also call for settler communities to initiate a form of self-transformation.

The question is how do we begin this self-transformation? Or put in a more sophisticated fashion, how do we become allies to Indigenous people without re-committing colonization in a different guise?

The answer for me is to begin to acknowledge, recognize, and explore the Other within.

Writing and the Sonic Landscape

The brown stain inside my coffee cup looks like birch bark. Tires rolling over asphalt. A hybrid taxi rolls to the light. Sparrows at my feet.

This place is more a hub of social activity than a coffee shop. And I am trying to write. Last night, I dreamed my mouth was full of blood.

I sit with three members of my writing club. We meet most mornings. The sky is faint. A warm morning. I am distracted again and again by just about everything.

This is writing.

Writing, where outcomes, deadlines, and word counts are set aside. You're supposed to let the writing come to you.

Ha.

My vacations concern writing. This behaviour defines me. Writing is how I catch up with myself, figure it out. I am also trying to describe the nextness of my life.

Rather than resisting the chaos of this busy cafe, I allow it to permeate the back of my neck and the bottom of my tongue.

There is a practice I am working on, a meditation in some respects, that you might call mindful writing. In mindful writing, your attention is focussed while your awareness is diffuse. Like composing a poem while speeding down the I5, one hand in your pocket.

When the writing goes well, I feel the pen moving across the prairie of my notebook while I attend to the sounds around me. Sparrows at my feet. Cappuccino tapping. The hazy wind across my past and future.

Sometimes, when you write, there is a very interesting thing that happens. The listening changes the words on the page. The sparrows – their skippy, hoppy essence – flit across my consciousness in a way that changes the moment.

A mouthful of blood. Merciless northern light. A satellite in orbit.

The pen moves. Thoughts unravel. My awareness seems to skip, like the jerky movements of birds, and time feels ready to fracture, like someone changing channels in the sky.

Reality is a train headed north, and I am in an orbit above it. I used to think that we were all on a train rushing toward the future. And you and I were sitting on the train together watching the world go by, seeing the houses we used to live in, remarking on the people we used to know. Wondering who will love us tomorrow and to what soundtrack.

I don't think that anymore.

In a dream, my father rides with me on top of trains. Mouths covered with handkerchiefs. Eye sockets grimy with soot. We ride to Seoul to sell vegetables.

Click. A nurse pulls a sheet over my face. My son is with me now. On my deathbed.

All time is one, he whispers.

* * *

My writing partner, Kelly, clears her throat and points to the green awning just east of the coffee shop.

"That's the schizophrenia society."

I look at the green door. It clicks to a close. I am no longer afraid of catching my father's schizophrenia. Just like I am no longer afraid of catching my mother's pancreatic cancer.

Life is not a train. Reality is not so linear as I imagine. These dreams are not lined up for me to experience like airplanes waiting to land.

Sometimes the nurse I see in my orbits above the single track of my life and death appears to be my daughter and sometimes my wife. Sometimes I see strangers, faces from other dreams.

Perhaps it is you?

You hold my hand. My mouth tries to move. I taste the loneliness of this hospice room. I see the oak picture frame surrounding a northern landscape.

I come from the spruce city. Loneliness is the worst and best of things. That's what the trees say. Loneliness, it must be said, is often the subject of my coffee shop writing. Perhaps it is the anxiety of marriage. Will my wife one day tell me she's had enough of my socks? And what about the prospect of the empty nest, my children making their own tracks and orbits?

How I love my children.

But whenever I feel this strange loneliness, I don't know what else to call it. I heed the words of my mentor, Pauline Oliveros, a great thinker of consciousness, who advises me to do one thing to live well: listen deeply.

We only have to listen, to meditate upon the sonic landscape, to hear, to really hear. Beyond identity, there is no loneliness.

Pauline, who I will meet for the first time this summer, is the founder of the Deep Listening Institute, a place where people explore listening as a way we can jump the tracks, discover new orbits, and perhaps even remember ourselves differently.

I have discovered that it is possible to lift yourself off the page, off the single track of existence, out of these bags of skin and become something.

"Listening changes you," says Pauline.

You are sitting at the coffee shop reading these words. Look at the shape of your compassion from high above. Feel the sun whispering upon your ethic.

Sometimes I can hear a faint vibration. Voices in the distance. The sound of spruce. Sparrows at my feet. The tragedy of our children.

Your parents are telling you how much they will always love you. In their voices is the reverberation of multiple universes and the echo of your ancestors inside a particle of light.

We used to hold on for the ride. Now we let go. Let go.

On Creativity

"Every act of creation is first of all an act of destruction."
Pablo Picasso

We have moved so many times that there are boxes I have yet to open. These darn boxes just get moved from house to house. I recently opened one of these boxes, and I found something that I didn't quite expect: my father's writing journal.

My father died a decade ago, and I must have packed up his journal in a blue binder along with all those things I couldn't bear to throw away: boxes of sermons, a manual typewriter, and theology books. This particular journal begins exactly twenty years ago in the summer of 1988.

In one poem he writes about me:

This is a poem about my son Stan.

Whom I have hurt a thousand

Times . . .

My father began the journal when he was 57 years old. He had tried to find another position as a United Church minister, but no church said yes. My parents lived in a one-bedroom condominium in Metrotown. He spent his days pursuing writing, driving my mother to and from work, and feeling lonely and useless.

He rarely shared much of his inner life with me, so his journal is a revelation. The words tell me a great deal about his despair, isolation, and fears. The journal also tells me a great deal about myself too, because in many ways my father's struggles are my own.

The sky may be blue, the water sparkling, and the sun warm, but there are many, like my father, who have difficulty escaping their darker emotions. We all have difficult feelings, but we also know sometimes it's difficult not to give in to despair.

My father's journal cries out desperately for creative expression. He writes that he never explored his creative potential. He saw this final stage of his life as an opportunity to explore what he calls *unborn* talent.

We all possess creative talent, and in many of us, there is a strong urge to be creative, to express ourselves in meaningful ways. I see these deep longings in everyone. No matter who we are or how old we are, we long to express ourselves.

But where to begin?

Well, maybe I should know. After all, I have been a creative person all my life. I chose a creative career and consider myself a creative professional which means I utilize a creative process in my work.

But all of us, those who write music, design objects, shape sculptures, click photographs, write novels, or put form to canvas, will tell you the same thing about creativity. It's about emotional risk, more specifically facing your fears.

I will tell you the honest truth: every time I face the blank page, I turn myself inside out. Creative people become expert at accessing their vulnerabilities. It's what allows the creation of serious long-lasting art. It's what allows the real truth to be uncovered. It's what makes being creative addictive, exhilarating, and painful.

Emotional risk is what I do as an artist. I pick away at memory. I focus intensely on what I don't understand. At my best and most courageous, I plunge into my own fears.

Of course, not all creative people are into this type of torture, but many understand in order to find truth and beauty, you have to work at it. I know many budding artists who want to produce that hit record, beautiful painting, or unforgettable screenplay without understanding the creative process requires one to be true to the landscape of soul, not the shrill of the marketplace.

Creative people, especially those who haven't yet found their medium, or a confidence in exploring their own sense of expression, often find it difficult to begin. After all, what is a more daunting task than facing the proverbial blank canvas?

If you want to put pressure on someone, tell him or her, "You're fortunate, you have the freedom to do or achieve whatever you want."

Instead, ask questions like, "What kinds of experiences have you had that filled with you with the most joy? What have you done in your life that occupied you to the maximum and made time melt away?"

Be careful not to discount anybody's answers to these questions. Being creative is absolutely not the province of what our society deems as artistically valuable. Any task can be accomplished with creativity.

An artist isn't someone who necessarily sells the work; an artist can be someone who pursues enlightenment through any task or activity. I have met artists who were engineers, teachers, gardeners, lawyers, parents, welders, and salespeople.

When it comes to expressing yourself as an artist, it's not what you do, but how you do it. Creative people often utilize a process that helps them explore ideas, choices, and questions.

My own process is really quite simple. First I write down as freely as possible every single possibility I can collect. I take this brainstorming phase more seriously than most. I have notebooks filled with brainstorming, clustering, note taking, and doodling.

The second phase is questioning. Without choosing a possibility, I begin to ask questions. Here is where you really have to listen to your feelings and not just your analytical side. I ask questions that have to do with assessing the depth of an idea or choice.

I ask myself what scares me the most.

I also look for things that others might throw away. For example, I consciously seek misunderstanding, confusion and doubt. These areas are like gold mines. What you think you understand is often the last place to find your treasure. Instead, go exactly where a person like you would never look.

The act of creation seems like the first stage to many, but it is really the last stage. My family knows an artist works at the oddest times and in the oddest ways. I take notes in the movie theatre. I speak into my tape recorder in the middle of the night. My wife will tell you that I, the grumpiest soul in the world, takes looking out the window very seriously.

Unfortunately, I never had a discussion with my father about these things. I read his journal now, and I feel how afraid he was about exploring his own soul. I wonder how many people out there want and need to explore their artistic potential. If you do, I encourage you to share your desire with someone you care about. Beyond fear, there is great freedom, accomplishment, and joy.

I Held My Breath for a Year

Moods: Signals from the Emotional Universe

I am in a mood about moods. My default mood is sort of distracted, and sometimes it's merely . . . annoyed. But right now my energy feels somewhat different. Something inside me skips a beat. Like air beneath a feathered wing, I feel lifted.

Wow, I'm suddenly in a good mood. In these moments of splendour, I am apt to hug you. Or ask you to exercise with me. Well, let's not get ridiculous!

Why do moods change as easily as the sky? Now, the world dims and the clouds brew. Enter anxiety. Descend criticism and its partner, judgement. Tell me, why do I sleep with my molars clenched? What is so taxing?

Is it the weather? Air pressure? The words of a certain someone? I am male. Aren't I socialized to be unfeeling?

Buck up. Sometimes we cannot afford for a mood to exist. So we act, or deny. Or run away. Or furiously consume.

Is there something more to our moods? Might our moods be telling us something?

If our condition is not medically serious, we should not run to self-medicate. Let us not bury feelings to have them appear as high blood pressure later.

A mood might be a signal, a beacon, a fire on a distant beach, an inkling of something valuable.

In short, moods can be an interesting form of intelligence. They can be as tantalizing and illusory as our dreams.

What kind intelligence do moods offer us?

Have you ever looked at a piece of art and had your mood changed? Have you ever walked into a forest and suddenly felt different? Have you ever inhaled fresh lavender and been moved?

Ask a designer, architect, or artist. There is a kind of rhetoric of moods.

Have you ever been altered by a poem? A song heard while shopping? A cup of peppermint tea? The fragrance of burning embers?

How are we altered by our moods? What exactly does seeing a monument or walking through a forest do?

It's as if the sound of my footsteps, smell of pine, and outline of winter branches against sky flips some kind of switch.

Allowing myself to be altered by these experiences has shifted me. What alters you?

The trees, mountains, poetry, music – they make me consider myself, my contribution, and my purpose.

Sometimes I notice other things, too. Like who I need to apologize to. Like how I can love better. Like how to be more accepting and open.

Being mindful of our variations of mood can help us think new thoughts, sense new feelings, but perhaps more importantly, alter who we are in the very moment of the moment.

I no longer view anger and anxiety as merely uncontrollable

stress. On the contrary, emotional stressors to our system are transformational signals on our emotional network. What happens when we become more open to the signal intelligence of our moods? For me, it is the difference between traumatic stress and traumatic growth.

When is the last time you allowed a mood or an emotion to not weaken you, but strengthen you? Not break your bones, but make them stronger?

How do we allow this consciousness to take place without allowing emotions to govern us?

Being sensitive can be painful, but without these receptors, we cannot accept the power of feeling deeply as a gift. We must strive to accept the signals of the emotional universe, no matter what someone else tells us to feel.

Perhaps we should welcome the unpredictable storm of our emotional lives and apprehend the spontaneous as beautiful and purposeful confusion. The flurry of our emotions can make us, if we are mindful, stronger, more able to contribute.

Let us say this to our children, parents, friends and even ourselves: I love you because you feel so strongly.

And finally, let us take this beautiful confusion, this symphony of emotions, and allow the storm to heal us of our need to control what we do not understand. Let our sensitivities alter us like the moon alters the oceans.

What would happen if we could learn to accept the Universe as not one thing or another, but many confused, beautiful, and irreconcilable fragments?

What do you feel? What is your mood?

There is beauty, joy, sadness, and heartbreak in every moment of our emotional universe.

This means that reading and responding to emotions has always been our task . . . the task of parenting. Of building peace. Of loving. Accepting. And discovering our shared universe.

Honest Feedback

One of things that I'm quite afraid of receiving is honest feedback. I love receiving dishonest feedback. "Hey, you're great. You're the best. You're not fat." But when someone sits you down for some honest feedback, it's about as fun as a visit to the outhouse in January.

Feedback, not to be confused with what happens when you point your microphone at an amplifier, generally makes me angry and disappointed. This is why teachers don't as a rule love hearing what students really think about them. When I was a teacher, I shoved my student evaluations into a file cabinet and waited until they disintegrated.

One time, I was on this field trip with a bunch of high achievers, and one of the fellows sat down beside me (I think this was day three or something), and said something to me very softly.

"Hey, would you please tell me what you think of me?"

Now this person was a courageous, creative, highly skilled professional. At least that's what I thought he wanted to hear. But he was also extremely sensitive, amazingly insecure in odd ways, and fairly demanding in an ego-driven way. Not that he couldn't stand up for someone else; he just liked to be right and in control. Who doesn't?

So, I sat there watching the yellow line on the stretch of Alberta highway. We were on a bus headed toward Banff and wondered how I could escape giving this person some dreaded feedback. So I only said some positive stuff and shut my mouth.

Was that the right thing to do?

I think he wanted me to say that I was impressed. The big honking ego that I walk around feeding said that maybe this guy just wanted Stan Chung's approval. After all, everyone wants my approval, I reasoned. It's part of my inscrutable Asian act. Nobody knows if I'm grimacing because I have painful stomach gas or whether I am trying not to laugh at you trying to use chopsticks.

I could have told him something constructive that he might actually improve, but all the recent strength theory says that nobody really wants to work on their weaknesses. There is no positive reinforcement when you work on stuff you're crappy at. Instead, we might as well apply our strengths and get better at things we're already good at.

Shining somebody's apple is something that I can do, if pressed, so I gave him a nice gush job. He was happy, and he found somebody else to sit beside. The strange part of this story is not how he felt, but how dissatisfied I felt. Really, I felt a little ripped off. Why?

Because I am such a fearful, gutless person that I neglected to ask him what he thought of me. Maybe he would have said something wonderful, which would have made me feel happy and deep down would have made me think he was a moron.

Maybe he would have said something that would blow my mind. Like maybe he could have said something that would feel like a shot to the head. Something I could reflect on, think about, and maybe thank him for in about 10 years, after I stopped brooding and feeling sorry for myself.

Instead, I just sat there.

What do people really think of you? I know you don't care, but does it matter? Does anyone actually know you and care enough about you to tell you something amazingly insightful?

Or do you only want to hear the good stuff? Do you only want to be stroked? After all, a little voice inside of you tells you how stupid and incompetent you are all day long. Accept a little praise and give yourself a break, you big baby!

A friend of mine despises this. He calls it childish handholding. Adults should not need to have their egos pumped up all the time. Some people, no matter how much appreciation they receive at work and at home, can't get enough ego pumping. They are always fishing for compliments, and I'm always getting hooked.

What is it about human beings that makes us crave appreciation so much?

I have a friend who drinks maybe a bit too much, forgets stuff, and conveniently ignores me and others whenever he feels like it. I know he's lost friends because of this. I know it affects his business, but do I have to be the guy to sit down with him and give him the big scary talk?

Forget about it!

Instead, I forgive him, complain about him, and consider myself lucky he doesn't do the same thing to me.

I've been told I'm arrogant, egocentric, righteous, and extremely manipulative. And that's from my friends. Actually, of all the criticism and feedback that I've received lately, the most hurtful, transformational, and insulting thing I've heard is that maybe I look a little lost.

It wasn't a hurtfully said thing, just a passing observation said in half jest. But I thought about it and decided that maybe I am lost. I don't know what I'm doing. I definitely don't ever know what I'm feeling. And most of the time, I forget to tell the people that I care about what I really feel about them.

Saying how you feel about someone is a much different thing than saying what you think. Saying what you think is an intellectual appraisal. A better approach, the approach I use when I consult my best self, is to feel the diamond part of that person, the highest sparkling version of that person and express how grateful you are for the jewel inside.

Using your heart is usually much better than using your head when it comes to the personal appraisal business. And if you don't know how to use your heart… well, it's never too late to stop grunting and say something.

Surprise yourself. Surprise a friend.

I have discovered something about you, you know? I have discovered that I'm really happy when I'm around you. I like being in your presence. You crack me up. There is something very precious about the way you . . . I just wanted to give you some honest feedback, ya know?

What Comes Between Us: The Secret of Secrets

We all think we know the *Secret*. There are many versions of it. Some people say that the secret is a kind of expectation: expect it and you will attract it.

What do you want to be? Well, you get what you attract, says the theory. Grumpy cynics get what they expect: positive dreamers, too.

Why not try faking it until you make it? That's another useful and probably related secret. Even academics are beginning to realize that the skills of life are best developed, not through reading or exercises, but through actual performance.

That is why *faking it* appears to be a useful way of building learning because *performing* is an authentic or real experience, not a simulated or theoretical one.

Some people believe in another kind of secret. They say that the ability to learn is truly the secret to life and success. Learning not only keeps our minds active, helps us stay employed, but is also a unique form of joy in itself.

Who doesn't love the feeling you get when you tilt your body into the wind and use learning to navigate your life and succeed?

Who doesn't love to learn?

Learning is not to be confused with schooling. In fact, sometimes you have to forget all your schooling in order to reconnect with your passion for learning.

Perhaps the *art of unlearning* is a kind of secret, too? Experts involved in the development of human potential often say that unlearning is part of the process of becoming more aware of how our boundaries and resistances have been constructed by our past and our culture. By unlearning some of our conventions, habits, and mindsets, we become more free, more able to be able to choose how we want to be in the world.

Learning is probably as important as breathing. But as we get older, our learning comfort zone tends to stay static or shrink, so it's important to surprise yourself and learn what a person like you would never learn.

It is good advice to determine a set of learning goals, but it might be even better advice to become more aware of your learning comfort zone.

What is your learning comfort zone? What is stopping you from learning?

For me, it is my own heart.

Love is often a topic that creates discomfort when it comes to the big secrets of life. A great many people consider love the secret – and the most challenging secret of all.

Our songs and stories are filled with little else, but our culture seems to be torn about love.

How do we attract love? How do we find the right kind of love? How do we learn to nurture love in a way that helps us grow as humans and enhance our relationships? How wonderful would it be if we unlocked the secret to love?

Could love be the biggest mystery of life?

For me, love is not always the answer. It can teach us to be passive and can make us feel helpless. Love can isolate us from what is real.

What, then, is the secret? Let's call it. . . dialogue.

If you know how to enter, build, and sustain a dialogue with another human being then you may know the secret.

Many know how to enter a dialogue, but they can't maintain it. Others know how to build dialogue, but the relationships flounder at the same points.

The lucky and the few know how to enter, build, and sustain a dialogue.

Such dialogues give us the deepest and most profound sense of joy. Religions are essentially dialogues. Our relationship to place is a dialogue. Marriages, too.

How do you assess whether you really know the secret?

An easy way is to examine your relationships. How many of your relationships are deep partnerships?

True, close, and deep partnerships are rare because they are essentially dialogues that are continually evolving and growing.

Dialogue is what makes a relationship grow. Authentic dialogue, the kind of dialogue where two are essentially helping each other co-evolve, is quite an exceptional practice, and it is actually that – a practice. Dialogue is something to value, schedule, and exercise.

Dialogue has three principles:

1. Story

Dialogue recognizes that each person has a story and each story has value.

2. Improvise Those in dialogue must not have a preordained purpose. The strategy of dialogue is to be open to influence, to be willing to be altered, to improvise.

3. Trust

Dialogue builds toward increasing levels of emotional, intellectual, and aesthetic risk; rather than fearing risk, dialogue creates deeper and deeper levels of trust.

What to avoid: The problem with many conversations is that they are so one-sided that they never become dialogues. Or they sound like two people talking at the same time. Or they are filled with self-interest and defending a position. Or they are built artificially with drugs or alcohol or gurus.

Dialogue is a selfless and compassionate approach to building a shared understanding with another human being.

And the art and heart of dialogue may the *biggest secret of them of all.*

If dialogue is the *Secret*, then what is the secret of secrets?

Why, it is listening, of course. The kind of listening that comes from a still, quiet, and ever present place.

Idiot's Guide to Arguing: The 5 Stages of Disagreement

We live in world of disagreement. We just can't seem to help it. Whether we are debating elections, new arenas, refugees, capitalism, or terrorism, we find ourselves in what feels like a battle for our lives. Disagreement ravages our communities like wild fire. Some live peacefully in debate and disagreement, but few manage to escape without burned friendships and families.

If we cannot learn to manage disagreement within our core relationships is it any wonder that our world rages in a constant battle? Anger, despair, rationalizing, distance, and dialogue are the five stages of disagreement.

They are not meant to contain the messiness of human emotions; instead, I offer these five stages to help better understand disagreement as a process, as pieces of a larger puzzle.

Stage 1

Anger cannot and should not be contained. We are humans and we get angry. We lash out. We defriend family members. We give up on people. We say hateful words. There is no disagreement that does not contain within it some emotion.

Acknowledging my anger is the first step to becoming aware of what anger can create and destroy. The key to anger is understanding what lurks behind it: fear and pain. Unexamined fear eventually hurts people.

Neuroscientists talk about the reptilian part of the brain that uses fear as fuel in extreme situations. Our brains literally shut off, and we move into action. The destructive power of anger can quickly turn to violence.

Advice: I acknowledge my anger, but I will not let it be my master.

Stage 2

Despair happens because we can feel betrayed when someone disagrees with us. We are upset because disagreement suggests a lack of partnership. The disloyalty hurts us. We mourn the loss of fidelity. Feelings of betrayal can make us despair at our loss, even if the relationship needed to end.

The key to despair is understanding it is very normal. At this stage I strive to differentiate the argument from the person. There is a point in every parent's life, for example, where the child must disagree with the parent, in order to demonstrate that the parent has raised an independent person.

Advice: I describe my feelings without intending harm. E.g. I say "I feel hurt" rather than insulting phrases that begin with the word, *you.*

Stage 3

Rationalizing is born of fear of losing an argument. It has its roots in the competitive ego. Someone has disagreed with us, so we must marshal better arguments to convince our fellow combatants. I call it rationalizing because often the emotional undercurrents may be driving a false logic that is not particularly analytical.

Rationalizing appears to be driven by logic, but it is usually driven by a desire to shame, humiliate, or retaliate. Seeing an argument from many sides is one effective way in which we can combat our rationalizing thoughts.

Advice: The more perspectives I can appreciate before criticizing, the wiser and more human I become.

Stage 4

Distance is an ambivalent stage because it can mean two things at once; it can mean reaching a kind of objectivity that allows us to be aware of our emotions, and it can also be, at the same time, a way of escape, a distancing from how we really feel and think.

The most powerful tools to balance the power of distance are breathing and gratitude. You can immediately find distance if you can find a way to breathe during a time of disagreement. When I take a breath, I am able to note the distance between my emotions and my authentic self. That distance enables me to achieve a sense of gratitude, to be able to see myself and monitor my emotions, and eventually, better handle disagreement.

Gaining distance from one's sense of disagreement can help us understand that ego and even our personal values can prevent us from gaining as many perspectives as possible.

Advice: Learn to spot the difference between an argument that rests upon a sense of superior values and an argument that sees differing values as uniquely situational and worthy of respect.

Stage 5

Dialogue doesn't mean you win the argument. It may mean that you begin to see the limitations of a win/lose paradigm. A win/lose paradigm is a characteristic of dichotomous thinking. It's a style of thinking that often marginalizes other perspectives and encourages a sense of extremes such as "My way or the highway or are you with me or against me?"

Dialogue is powerful when we realize that fear, ego, and/or pain are often linked emotionally to our core values. Any growth in perspective requires managing our emotions because we are threatened when our values are challenged. For example, new ideas on human rights and equality for minorities have challenged our perceptions of how we think about ourselves and the world.

Dialogue is a powerful way to achieve knowledge that goes beyond rightness and wrongness. We discover that competing values can co-exist, that different people have a right to hold different values, and that our own sense of values is often more malleable than we realize. It is a sign of intelligence and maturity that we consider ourselves open to change as we grow and incorporate more perspectives.

Strange and wonderful things can happen when disagreement becomes dialogue.

Take a breath, glimpse yourself moving from defending an argument to engaging in creative dialogue. What happens when you monitor your emotions and they no longer master you? What happens when you watch yourself listening and withholding judgment?

The world changes when disagreement becomes dialogue. The world changes when we resist fear and pain.

What's Better Than a Job?

A *regular* job used to be all you needed in life. But for two decades now jobs have been changing. And right beneath our noses. POOF! Jobs have changed.

A report from Morgan Stanley using OECD data shows Canada as one of the world leaders in crappy jobs. (http://www. huffingtonpost.ca) Most of us either work for someone or we're surviving on investment income. Some of you have more than one job. A small but growing group of you are doing something entirely different.

You may not realize this, but you could be leading us into a wild future where the once mighty job may become endangered. You might think that I am being nostalgic when I talk about the old steady, regular job. No, I am not. Many of those jobs exploited (and still do) our once abundant natural resources for short term profit.

We all know that our country has achieved great wealth. It is harder to admit that our environmental impact may not be survivable.

The old job is tough to come by. A study by the Conference Board of Canada says that young people are being paid levels that are historically low. http://www.conferenceboard.ca/e-library/abstract.aspx?did=6510

Perhaps we should think differently about work. There is a

different kind of economy emerging that turns the old notion of a job upside down. And it may even lower our standard of living (less income), raise our lifespans (more local food), reduce our consumption (more sharing), and evolve new political entities (citizen-controlled).

My brother-in-law, Charles, has a very good Okanagan life. He sails. Reads books. He eats well, but he has no *official* job. His income exceeds his expenses. And his expenses are ultra-low.

He is definitely not caught up in materialism. What gets him excited is what he calls Wanting Less Than You Already Have. He eats from the gardens of his neighbours in exchange for carpentry. He uses peer-to-peer websites to rent out their basement to tourists.

"When we have earned enough money that month by renting the suite, we sometimes just close up, and take a break from it," he said. "We work to live. Not the other way around."

Many people no longer work official jobs anymore. They have jumped off their big mortgages, cable bills, cell phones, and leased BMWs and are now engaged in an alternative economy.

Cy, one of my friends from childhood, lives in Brandon and has a part-time crap job. Also, he owns a graphics design business and sells collectibles on eBay when he needs cash.

He and his wife are content. Cy loves to fish and cheer for the green and white. They raised two kids in a 93m³ (1,000 sq ft) house that is fully paid off.

"It wasn't easy, and it's still challenging," Cy says. "You really want what other people have. But we wanted something more . . . a kind of freedom."

A friend from Vancouver designs and sells handmade jewelry on Etsy; a collaborative trading platform for artists and craftspeople.

Naomi, too, talks about freedom.

"My father had three weeks of vacation a year for 30 years," she says. "I cherish the time I spend with my daughter. I feel like I own my own time. With my website and other peer-to-peer sites, I don't have to do what my father did and trade so much of my life for money."

My own son and daughter remark they are learning a lot from my insistence that there are other ways to earn a living.

"A job is not our greatest asset: our freedom is," I say. "Can we forge an alternative economy?"

"Are you still free?" Charles asks me in a Skype conversation. "Or did you get shackled up with a job yet?"

"I don't know," I say laughing. "How are you?

"I work a few days every month," Charles says, as he looks out at his view of Okanagan Lake. "I might work a bit more if we need it. There is no one telling me what to do but me."

I have another friend who has a very good income, and she does not have an official job either. She and her family have no debt. They own two homes: one a 4-bedroom, 3-bathroom in Penticton; another, a modest 3-bedroom duplex in Thunder Bay.

They live in Thunder Bay and live on $3200 net income per month from their other home and $800 net from duplex. $4000 is the extent of their monthly income beyond the little social cooperative they run to help people figure out how to make a living, not individually, but cooperatively.

The two of them (and their children) are not tied to bosses and 40-hour work weeks.

"We live for relationships and to help change the world," they say. "We try to model for our children what true civic engagement looks like. We think society has forgotten what an economy is for."

Is there a better way, a large scale alternative to the job?

Many look to the Basque region of Spain to a worker-owned cooperative called Mondragon. The values-driven co-op employs 75,000 people in finance, industry, retail, and knowledge sectors. They make car parts, run stores, and operate a university. Last year they produced approximately $16 billion US in revenue. (en. wikipedia.org/wiki/Mondragon_Corporation)

They are not perfect at Mondragon. But the employees don't exactly have crap jobs. They happen to be owners.

Some call it the Collaboration Economy. Others call it Enlightened.

Catch

and Release

"To everything there is a season,
and a time to every purpose under the heaven:
A time to be born, and a time to die; a time to plant,
and a time to pluck up that which is planted."
Ecclesiastes

She bit her lip with concentration. My nine-year-old girl balanced in the canoe. Her black hair moved in the breeze and settled on the collar of her life jacket. She held a fishing rod that bent at the tip as I paddled.

In the distance, spires of black spruce stood against the waist of the sky. Now that it was finally July, the sun had regained its heat.

Coolness rose off the water. I felt we were moving through the Universe as one even though the Universe is just this small lake above Peachland surrounded by craggy trees. It's summer again, I said to myself. She was nine years old, and this day was to surround and pass us as surely as the water swirled around the blade of the paddle.

In September on a bright Sunday, I held her small hand as we explored the spawning channels at Mission Creek Regional Park. The parking lot is crowded; there are exhibits to explore.

We entered the log museum and learned about the life cycle of the land-locked sockeye known as kokanee. We walked and talked about how this delicate and threatened creature fits so perfectly into the cycle of life, not just its own cycle from egg, alevin, and fry, to smolt and fingerling but how the kokanee spawn, die, and are consumed by animals or returned to the soil as nutrients for other forms of life.

"These kids," my wife said to me that day, "they know more than we think."

The next night at dinner, we each took turns discussing our Monday.

"Did you ask any questions today?" I asked. We still find it very amusing that both our children like to raise their hands at the dinner table.

"Yes, Clementine?" I said with a mouthful of stroganoff. "You can put your hand down now."

"I asked her a question, and Daddy, I bet you can't guess what she said to me."

"I don't know. What did your teacher say?" I asked.

"Well, we talked about kokanee today and my teacher said she didn't even know the answer to my question!"

"Really? So what did you ask your teacher?"

"I asked her why the kokanee die after they lay their eggs. So, why do they die?"

"Well, honey, hmm, gee, that's an excellent question," I said wondering what to say next.

"I guess nobody knows the answer to that one," said my wife.

I glanced at Clementine. We named her after the delicately-skinned orange that her mother craved when she was pregnant.

Clementine's brown eyes nearly exploded with curiosity at the thought of her question.

Why did the kokanee die? I had no explanation. Why did this small fish who struggled so heroically against the odds in order to return to its origins and lay its eggs conclude its journey with . . . well, with death?

I remembered a few years back walking along Deep Creek at Hardy Falls Regional Park near Peachland. The red carcasses of exhausted worn out fish were strewn everywhere along the creek, the smell of rotting flesh inescapable. It looked like a massacre. I couldn't stand the sight or the stench or the true meaning of it all. I ended up running down the path to escape. I told the kids Daddy was just exercising.

After dinner and a bath, I kissed her cheek and held my lips against her soft skin. "Good night, little girl. You're the best little girl in the world."

"And you're the best daddy in the whole wide world. You have a good sleep, too. I love you."

I wished for a moment that I could stop her from growing up, that I could, with the force of my puny human will, freeze her just as she appeared before me. A beautiful little girl poised at the beginning of an awakening. I wanted to keep her from growing up, protect her from losing the miraculous sense of wonder we can feel especially at this time of year.

Last weekend, we did as we always do at this time of year. We drove to our favourite farm on the Rutland bench. We stumbled out of the van, as eager as any family could be. It was time to pick grapes. Big, fat, luscious grapes, grown under the hot summer sun.

We ducked under the vines, as we always do, and stood beneath them. It was so quiet under there. Black globes hung above us in huge pendulous clusters. Tight triangular spheres, dusky and filled with heavenly juice. The light beneath a grapevine, if you have not experienced it, is simply miraculous.

I have never been to the great cathedrals of Europe, nor stood before the paintings of the renaissance masters, but I imagine that the light could be no more holy, no more profound that the light filtering through an Okanagan grapevine.

My daughter gripped her bag of grapes and ran through the vineyard. This girl, she runs for no reason. She loves life. This girl twitches when she is standing still. She vibrates with energy. She leaps out of bed in the morning and tumbles into bed at night with glee. Without her, we would not live in quite the same way, not in the special way she teaches us.

When Clemo was a baby, I spent hours trying to rock her to sleep. My legs would cramp, my shoulders would sag. I would think, like all fathers before and after me, that there was nothing more precious, no honour more glorious, than the privilege of being her father.

The fall reminds us of good things, and the quiet routine of life. Things ripen. Things are harvested. The peaches were good this year, weren't they? The cherries were elusive and sweet, like living chocolate. We loved our trips to buy fruit and pick fruit at local orchards. We found a farm in Armstrong last spring with tender asparagus. Those asparagus sweetened our hearts as did the plump bright tomatoes fattening in the hot corner of our yard.

There is a wild sensuality in eating with the seasons. Especially in this region where the bounty of local farms and our own gardens remind us that we are people of the earth, people who know deep in our genetic code that we are connected to nature. We know that we are nurtured and educated by the richness of the soil, the clarity of the water, and the passing of the seasons.

This season I will marvel at my little girl running through orchards. I will remember her telling us the story of the kokanee. I will watch her this year, as I did last year, and the year before, as she piles up the yellow leaves that have fallen from the sky. She will pile them up and jump in.

She will do it again and again. She will laugh with her brother. We will wave from the window. And we will try not to cry.

This time of year can make our ancient instincts come alive. These instincts arise despite the fact that we live comfortable and modern lives. A hundred years ago, before modernity, and maybe even centuries before when all we had were campfires, your kin and perhaps my kin would tend to their plants and await harvest.

Perhaps a long time ago, a long lost ancestor of yours or mine, would walk along a creek much like the one we call Mission Creek and wonder about the red fish. They would wonder, as we wonder now, why these fish spawn and then give up their lives. Yes, so that life can go on and on. So that our daughters will grow and show us that we will live on, too, even after the fall.

Don't Even Try to Understand

"Lighten up while you still can.
Don't even try to understand."
The Eagles

Easy love. Easy job. The easy life. What if life were just a bit darn easier? The commute shorter. The squabbles fewer. The money easier to earn. What if your life were 20% easier? What would you trade for more easy?

We want easy jobs, but easy jobs do not pay great. The flow of easy money depends on the river of life, on intelligence and talent. Smart people can patent their inventions. Talented people have to wake up to working hard. And hardworking people have to learn to let go.

Talent takes you to first base. Education takes you to second. Hard work to third. Home runs are all about what Pauline Oliveros calls Quantum Improvisation, making the impossible become easy by letting go of our constraints.

How do we make the impossible become easy?

We know one thing: getting to easy is never easy. Practice is essential. Educating yourself takes discipline and determination. Figuring out your path whether you're 25 or 50 requires a commitment to one important task: regularly listening to yourself.

Want easy happiness, love, money, knowledge, more expertise? No matter what kind of easy you want, you won't go far in any dimension without self-reflection.

For some, success means easier relationships. One where things are calm and you pretty much get what you want. Easy relationships can last forever; or they can crack as soon as the going gets tough.

A relationship is a shared investment. I've learned the hard way that low maintenance is good for cars, but not for serious relationships. How well are you maintaining your important relationships?

Work is all about relationships. Some people lose their jobs because people say they are not easy to work with. Do you know someone who does not understand what easy to work with means? Are you easy to work with?

"I have to be me," we loveable losers explain. "Why couldn't they accept me the way that I am?" We are entirely social creatures. Being tossed out of the herd is painful, especially if you don't get it.

Being yourself in our culture is two things: it's an excuse for being a brazen idiot/hero or it's a way of fitting in without getting stoned to death. Different cultures vary in the strength of the herd factor. The Canadian dominant culture is very tolerant as long as you dress conventionally, use polite words, speak clearly, chew with your mouth closed, mow your lawn and/or keep your deck neat.

We like to think that people who don't fit in make our lives less easy, so difficult people are easy to blame. Difficult problems cause us to run for the easiest solution. And the easiest solution of all? Blame someone else.

Ask anyone who went to residential school, internment camp,

or who fled their first country because of oppression. Blaming is an incredibly important phase, but it can also be problematic with respect to healing.

The blame process is common at work as well. The higher you go up at work, the more you see the Teflon people who never accept responsibility when the ride gets bumpy.

Check out the blame game at the bars and clubs. If you are in the dating scene, you'll see many souls stumbling from one relationship to another. You may be too eager or too passive, too affectionate or too much a prude; whatever it is, it is so much easier not to blame yourself.

On the other hand, we have a culture that systematically teaches us that individuals are solely responsible for their fate. Children grow up believing they caused their parent's divorce. Adults with addiction issues grow up believing they caused their own childhood trauma. Your childhood is not your fault.

Life would be a lot easier if we stopped blaming others for what we did wrong. It would be even easier if we stopped blaming ourselves for things we didn't do. The easiest thing of all in our culture might just be the most difficult: being alone with only ourselves. Being easy on yourself is one thing; it might be even more challenging to be easy with yourself.

No, that doesn't mean buying stuff and chasing it down with sugar. Being easy with yourself is taking the time to accept that what you're doing right now is probably what you really want to do.

Being easy with yourself is forgiving yourself for your mistakes and seeking forgiveness from others as well, even if they are no longer around.

Being easy with yourself, most of all, is taking the time to listen to your thoughts. This isn't about goal setting and dreaming about celebrity. It is more about self-observation and what Oliveros calls Deep Listening.

What is on your mind? How are you feeling? What thoughts and feelings are moving across the sky of your being? What story are you telling yourself right now?

Are you ok? Do you need to take a breath? Can listening deeply to your thoughts make your life easier?

Yes. It's easy, if you try.

Be exhorted by the rhythm of your breath. Be invited to do the impossible. Take it easy.

Growing Up Before Our Children Do

"The heart has its reasons of
which reason knows nothing."
Blaise Pascal

The bruise on my mother's thigh is the colour of a prairie sunset and as big as my fist. He's hurt her again, I think. I am only 11 years old. Wrist bones like a bird. I pledge in my heart that my father will not hurt her again. I lay awake at night promising the stars a double-barreled blast of vengeance.

A hot summer day. She is taking driving lessons from him. They are in the dry fields at Chimney Lake. Grasshoppers float above trampled grasses. Loons in the distance. Dust. She is learning to shift the Mercedes. She stalls. The car lurches. His ears brighten into hot coals.

When she misses a shift, the transmission grinds, and I can see him forever pinching her thigh, twisting deeply, unable to control the fury. She closes her eyes and bites the inside of her mouth.

When I am 16, she shows me another bruise. This time a dark plum upon her arm. I'm ready to fight back now. I am taller, stronger, and more prepared than ever.

I understand him better now or so I believe. He has slapped me, twisted my arm, thrown me around. Just like her, he is my saviour and tormentor. And while I am scared, (this is a man with a black belt, this man who has raised me) I am ready to move forward with his same fury.

Oh, the great unpredictable storm. At the age of 16, I never knew what I would find when I got home for school. Every day, every damn day, I would trudge up to my front door, open it, and listen. Was she alive? If it was too quiet, I would imagine her figure affixed on the floor or merely scrubbing it on her knees. If I heard the TV or kitchen sounds, then I would appear upstairs lost in my nonchalance. At dinner, we never knew what to expect. Nobody did. For the golden century of our childhood, we tiptoed.

The adult in me says this is the normal behaviour of someone who was not raised properly. These are the signs of someone in trouble. The adult in me says you have to understand a person like this. The child in me screams something else.

As a teenage boy, I grew up preparing myself for three things: girls, university, and homicide. I rehearsed all three. Just like athletes preparing for a big game by mentally rehearsing and imagining a victory. I did the same thing. There he is now, I would point to the police with my knuckles on fire, that person splayed awkwardly, the one not moving.

I don't know how many sons think of their fathers in this way. This is not friendly rivalry. When I got older, things didn't get necessarily better. I moved to Toronto and never looked back. When I returned my father slipped into another role. He got older, weaker and more dependent upon my mother. His anger subsided and turned into something else.

And then another thing happened: I contemplated my mother's

part in all of this.

When I was six years old, I watched her toss her wedding ring down the drain. I saw her tear up her wedding dress. How does a six-year-old say this to his mother: "You can divorce him. I'll take care of you."

How does a six-year-old process his mother's suffering? How bad must it have been to turn to your child in this way? I played the starring role as my mother's protector and confidant. I grew up believing I had a rescue mission. To free my mother. Is this what all sons believe?

Sometimes I think marriage is no place for a child. The ebb and flow of adult concerns have no business inside the imagination of a child. Children know when things are not good; they can feel it. But the only role they should ever play is that of child, not confidante, not friend, not emotional crutch and certainly not hero.

I will never say to my child, "You take care of your old man/old lady for me, okay?" I will never say to my child, "You're the lady/man of the house." Who is supposed to lean on whom?

And yet there are many signals in our culture that demonstrate how we have infantilized parents and sexualized children. Children grow up as caregivers to parents who can't sustain themselves emotionally, morally, or financially. We listen to our children as if their innocence and naivety will be our guide. The typical family sitcom is a living testimony to the construction of the child as a wisecracking all-knowing sage bent on parental re-education.

We say, *please child, give us a clue.*

The market sees children as the best and only place to spend advertising dollars. Get them hooked on a brand now, and you'll see loyalty for a lifetime. Our popular culture reinforces the idea that children are only miniature adults. Their experiences are validated by our nostalgic obsession for our own Disney childhoods. Too many of us try to grow up living through our children or behaving as if we are still children.

There is no group more vulnerable or more lucrative or more eager to please.

Her bruises have healed. There is no more pain. When I think about my parents now, I don't just see a cycle of pain. I think of the good times. I think of tender times. I think of how much I need them now, as fellow travelers on this blue and beautiful journey.

I think about how lost I feel without them. But what do I do about my murderous heart?

We loved each other. We hurt each other. We parented each other. We did the best we could in the time that we lived. In some ways, each of us is still lost.

May our children be raised by grownups. May childhood be preserved for our children.

An Idiot's Guide

to the

Canadian Economy

In Canada, we have three basic economic spheres that correspond with three types of employers: business, government, and community. If you understand these separate, yet interconnected spheres, you might just figure out recessions or who deserves your vote.

The dominant employer is business. Businesses depend upon demand for their products and services. There are many businesses. Most of them are not in manufacturing or resources, but in what Statistics Canada calls, services. Over 70% of Canada's businesses are classified as a service.

How is the service sector doing? Does it pay well? If you want more insight look at businesses who are giving their employees raises over the long term.

Don't look at mining, forestry, government, or manufacturing for raises. Look at the trading side of the service sector, more specifically at banks and financial services. These employers are some of the fastest moving and most competitive in the world.

Why? One reason is that the Canadian financial services industry is actually built upon sound government policy.

The second biggest employer in the economy is also the most complex player. Whether federal, provincial, or municipal, government doesn't just represent up to 30% of the jobs, but it remains an important spender and investor. The key to understanding government is determining where the spending and tax incentive priorities are.

In Canada, the major political parties do not vary wildly on their spending priorities or tax incentive schemes.

For example, all parties wish to invest heavily in post-secondary education. We make public spending a priority because education is correlated with prosperity, but also happiness and health (well-being). Our collective values also direct our parties to invest in an expensive public health care system.

Health care costs are obviously related to our collective health. And I don't know about you but stress, particularly financial stress, is hurting a lot of us. Not only is financial stress bad, but our diets have been influenced by those intent on selling us sugary food that is addictive and literally sickening.

Not only do we consume what puts us in hospitals, but I have to wonder, why do we have one sphere of the economy (i.e. fast food business) driving up costs in another sphere of the economy (publicly funded health care)?

Citizens everywhere are asking for a bold rethink. How are health and capitalism related? If cancer, heart disease, depression, and addiction are the price of being a G7 nation perhaps we should join a healthier club?

The third sphere of the economy may tell us a lot about how we might better balance the forces of capitalism with our need for collective and individual well-being.

The community sector (which includes non-profits) may form less than 20% of the jobs in the economy, but it is growing. Non-profits are not only turning out to be some very interesting employers, but they are contributing to the GDP in novel (often difficult to measure) ways.

What is an example of a non-profit job? Typical jobs include community school teacher, band nurse practitioner, economic development officer, church music director, new media journalist, social media coordinator, chamber of commerce director, and literacy director, to name a few.

Some community organizations are hiring game designers to devise social games created not to make profit, but to educate or impact social trends. It can be argued that social innovation will be responsible for the majority of our social issue breakthroughs (issues often exacerbated by capitalism), creating rewarding career paths for many.

The community economy isn't big enough to compete with the government and business economies; however, it provides much of the inspiration and innovation for both. Nearly all inventions that get patented and commercialized originate from the community, not from business or government.

The sports, fashion, and design industries find their inspiration from community, from trends developed by ordinary people. The global design industry depends for its inspiration on marginalized artists who may not always realize that their work is being *borrowed*.

Government and business can abuse the community economy. Businesses and governments have been accused of evading their ethical responsibility. For example: who cares for the young and old in your community? Who runs your local food bank?

Incidentally, why are so many middle class people regularly using food banks in Canada? Another G7 phenomenon?

So the smallest sphere of the economy may actually make the most difference in our lives, especially if we depend on things like product innovation, credit union services, child care, cooperatives, education, local food, and entertainment.

Local arts entertainment, for example, provided by independent musicians, writers, artists, painters, designers, and actors can create the sense of a meaningful life by inviting us to find pleasure in joy and reflection.

Local arts groups are endlessly struggling for breath because we are so accustomed to mass culture. I confess I often confuse watching hockey and Netflix on TV or playing silly on Facebook as actually meaningful living.

In whose interest is it to have us sedated with franchised consumption and mass culture? In whose interest is it to have our lives become so commoditized that we accept leaders that blatantly sacrifice our collective humanity for private greed?

In whose interest is it that we are tempted not to vote because corporatization has corrupted government to the extent that we can't see real differences in the major parties.

Finally, what is the relationship between the economy and the sense that we are truly free? Are we free to live our lives? Are we free to direct our governments? Are we free to demand from our businesses and governments what we really need in our communities?

The honest and bold idiot asks, what is an economy for? Education, more than anything, ought to examine what makes life worth living. An economic system in a democracy is judged easily, says this idiot: how does our economy work to promote well-being for all.

Canada Needs a Reliable System of Innovation

The Conference Board of Canada says that "despite a decade or so of innovation agendas and prosperity reports, Canada remains near the bottom of its peer group on innovation, ranking 13th among the 16 peer countries." http://www.conferenceboard.ca/hcp/details/innovation.aspx

Canadian business leaders say in surveys they don't know how to innovate and rate their innovation skills as average.

What happens if we don't innovate? It's a slow economic death spiral that will result in Canada's famed quality of life going backward.

Innovation can be defined as the ability to create unique products, services, and processes that have measurable value in the marketplace. There are many ways to measure innovation, but conventional wisdom believes innovation is best measured by dollars of new revenue as an output.

For example, a general rule of thumb is that 10% of an organization's revenue should be NEW every year. (Other measures of innovation include number of patents, number of start-ups, research investment, and access to capital investment.)

New ideas on innovation metrics focus less on output and more on human input factors such as internal capability, innovation intensity, and sector collaboration.

Most Canadian organizations do not have an innovation strategy or an innovation plan. On the other hand, strategic plans are filled with the vocabulary of innovation. The words are there, but the culture, reliable systems, processes, and strategies, are not.

An important way of thinking about innovation is seeing it as the development of a culture not just a set of imperatives or nice sounding words.

So if you're a school, band office, start-up, non-profit, government department, or a big company what should you do to kick-start your culture of innovation?

Here are seven steps to get you started.

It Starts at the Top

The leaders must be aligned on the importance of innovation to the organization. Without executive alignment, most innovation programs will fail.

My recommendation: do it in two weeks, boil it down to one page, and be done with what is normally a long process. Secret tip: it starts with the boss walking the talk.

Think System, Not Silo

Many executives think that working on the system is a waste of time. True, in most organizations the parts rarely work together well, but with today's competition and instability, nothing can beat the power of one integrated platform. Unfortunately, Senge's systems thinking is not an easy thing to learn. My recommendation: learn to be ruthless about investing only in those processes that add value. Being strategic means stop doing everything.

Transform the Culture

Economic guru Peter Drucker said that culture eats strategy for lunch. Of course, both are important. Middle managers are weary of eating the yuck sandwich known as change. The best kind of change is nurtured from customer experience. The best way to change? Virally. Small inoculations. Make it easy, painless, and without fear.

My recommendation: Give your best people an opportunity to test their best ideas over a two-week period and then invite them to pitch their concepts to leadership.

Embrace Trial and Error

There is nothing worse than an organization paralyzed by fear of failure. As guru Doug Hall says, fail fast and fail cheap. The more you fail through low risk experiments and live trials, the sooner you will make those game-winning advances and create Taleb's radical notion of *anti-fragility* – a culture/person that thrives under stress.

Innovation Comes in Three Flavours

Experts like Hall call regular innovation CORE. Core is continuous improvement. And then, there is game-changing and disruptive innovation which he calls LEAP. I suggest long term value comes in creating PLATFORM innovation. Platform innovation is a learning space for diverse stakeholders to discuss systems level issues and business model challenges.

Rethink the Aversion to Patents

I work with Canadian companies who receive licensing revenue through their intellectual property. A US patent costs less than $400. It can take less than 30 days to secure and can give you the kind of protection you need to develop innovations that are uniquely yours. Patents seem to be important everywhere but in Canada.

IT is It!

Do you want to know the ONE thing that will yield results? What is the *minimum effective dose* for low risk max value? It is the number of internal IT people employed to create unique value through your website. eCommerce activity is a useful proxy measure of innovation. Is your website a pretty brochure or a place to test and drive *mission critical* experiments?

The United States uses Canadian start-ups as a farm team for interesting new companies to purchase and often relocate. Today, most big companies buy start-ups to secure new ideas that have been pre-tested and already protected. Canadian companies are swallowed up every day by these companies often making rock star millionaires of entrepreneurs.

But jobs often move south because Canada doesn't necessary have the environment for global success in a time of great pressure and dwindling government research investment.

You can solve short term pressures by cutting jobs and instituting efficiency processes like Lean. Efficiency can yield you maybe a 4% gain at best. But compare this to a LEAP innovation: Apple introduced the iPad, and in a few short years it represented 60% of their total revenue.

I have great hope for a better understanding of platform or business model innovation. This kind of innovation is already helping Canada's aerospace, agriculture, and clean-tech sectors.

Innovation is complex. It works through a process conventionally called the Innovation Pipeline. The first phase is Idea Creation or Discovery. The second phase is Idea Development. The third phase is Idea Commercialization or Deployment.

All three phases must be integrated.

Canada's innovation pipeline depends on our schools, aboriginal bands, colleges, universities, industries, governments, non-profits, regions, cities, external partners, and communities, all working in concert.

The evidence from the United States is crystal clear. The innovation pipeline requires government vision. Let's imagine an education/research system that spurs more discoveries, a deep investment fund that nurtures the most novel companies, and an integrated innovation culture that employs thousands.

Unfortunately, our pipeline is not producing. It is time to innovate Canada's system of innovation.

Hot Summer in Your Town

Cranbrook is enjoying a hot and dry summer. I'm off for two weeks, so we thought we'd drink on the deck, swim at the lake, and ride a bike to Kimberley. Later in August, we plan on doing some *serious visiting*.

Are you up for a visit? Normally, we plan our vacations around destinations. San Francisco. Maui. Spokane. But this year, we aren't visiting places, we are visiting . . . people. We miss our favourite people. Like you. Sort of.

There is probably an art to visiting people which explains why I am not good at it. First of all, asking to stay at your house is a delicate matter. What if you say no? What if you say yes?

How is it that a house guest can turn into a mortal enemy in a matter of days? Did I ever tell you your house kind of smells like cabbage soup mixed with dryer sheets? Oops, did I say that aloud?

This is why I like to stay at hotels or campsites, so you don't have to experience me as the *guest from hell*. I confess that I am probably too old to sleep in your musty basement. Perhaps I am too old to wear my pajamas in front of you?

I admit it. I am not good at making myself at home at your home. So, we'll hotel it and come visit. I will try not to drink all your fine booze and eat your good cheese, if you promise not to cross your legs wearing that house coat again.

While we won't be in your basement listening to your snoring or midnight spousal manoeuvers, chances are we are still dying to see you. Time flies. Kids grow up. Life tilts in different directions. Our eyes weaken. We run marathons until hip surgery.

We become different people. We tolerate less from our guests. Yes, I'm afraid of what you'll think of me; my restlessness, obsessive reading, penchant for kim chee and involuntary poverty.

Yes, I'm pretty much the same. Just older and less loving of people who are certain of their certainties. My gray hairs are noticeable from across the room. Reading glasses dangle around my neck. I can read prescriptions, and it makes it impossible to hug me.

But we are so glad to see you. So much has changed in the last five or ten years. We've had job scares. Medical scares. Rapid weight loss and gain. Stints in the hot yoga ward. The world may be hectic, but nothing has hit us harder than attending a loved one in a hospital room, or standing helplessly in a funeral home, or that modern tragedy of tragedies – the unanticipated Facebook defriending. Sorry about that. We feel your loss. We really do.

What is the protocol for telling someone that you'd love to visit, but cannot stomach their views on Facebook?

Why did we lose touch? Truthfully, we've forgotten what we've done to you or what you've done to us.

Let us bury the hatchet. I can't quite recall the offence. What are you annoyed with me about, a lousy few thousand bucks? That thing with your boss? Or the matter of holy matrimony?

Well, our fault. Our fault. We moved away. We truly miss our city friends. Our Vancouver and Victoria pals never see us. Hey, it is the big city curse: parking is that difficult.

I wonder why cities have lost their fascination with us. Why does going to Vancouver feel like a colonoscopy?

And we simply don't have the finances necessary for travel on BC Ferries. Certainly, Vancouver Island has virtually everything except earthquake safety and affordability.

We can't wait to see our friends in our beloved Okanagan. There is nothing wrong with Kelowna, as long as you don't mind a little congestion and resetting your internal clock. Folks in the Okanagan wake up at 5 a.m. and go to bed before 9 p.m. This is primarily to avoid traffic.

Inevitably, during our visits I will drink a little bit more than usual. I should apologize in advance for my habits. Make sure you take care of your guests. A good bathroom fan is like gold.

Did you know we live in a small town now? Unfortunately, I simply can't tolerate urban density or line ups of any kind. In my town, it feels like zombie Albertans have killed off nearly everyone and left only truck owners. Ah, rural life. I love the wilderness of empty parking lots.

Isn't it time to visit friends this summer? Isn't it time to sit down with people who have known you for a long time? We can look into each other's gray whiskers and express what you've learned after all this time. That life isn't about sex, money, or real estate.

No, life is about knowing someone well enough to see their flaws and love them anyway. It's about them looking at you with that sense of wonder that can only mean there is something stuck in your teeth or that your zipper is down.

A wise person once said to me that you can't make new old friends. You can try, but your old friends know what you were like when you had flamboyance and a working short term memory.

If your friends are anything like my friends, a hot summer can be the best time to visit. On a fragrant evening with a glass of chilled wine everything can stop. For a second. And you can glance around. And everything and everyone is forgiven. Sort of.

Bring on the summer. We'll be there soon.

The

One Thing

Escalating food and gas prices. You struggle to keep your head above water. Speaking of water, an oil spill suffocates life at the bottom of the Gulf of Mexico. The Middle East crackles with civil war. In Japan, a nuclear nightmare.

Our planet remains gripped by environmental and human turmoil. What to do? What can we do?

How about meditate? What a sick joke. What can meditation do? How can meditation save lives? How can meditation pay the bills, bring home the bacon, and cool reactors?

Meditation, some say, solves nothing. It is a luxury, a fabrication of the *yoga class*, invented to deal with ego stress and false consciousness.

False consciousness is the deep slumber we live in, the matrix, a consumer culture driven by an economic agenda, which is controlled by no one, but somehow controls everyone.

If you've got dough, why bother waking up?

Jobs, we say. We need jobs. We need moula. We need productivity. Our economic reality must come first. It is self-evident, we say. Our economic model, the one needed for constant growth, consumption, and productivity has been bought and paid for by this planet.

If the planet is symbolized by the fate of the tree, then we have cut down that tree, used it, replanted it, and now that seedling suffers because the air burns, water boils, and soil mourns.

How could we as a species spoil our most basic gifts? How is it we not do realize that our precious economic model has poisoned our children and ourselves?

And what happens to those that question the way things are? Their voices rise shrill until they are consumed by our disgust. We cannot stop. We silence those who stand up for clean air, water, soil and freedom for other forms of life.

A moment of silence will not free us from our greed, ambition for wealth, and misguided desire for endless growth. Meditation will not do anything but make us conscious of our breath, our bodies, and our frantic inability to sit still.

Why can't I be alone with myself?

Meditation will not free us from ourselves, our creatively impotent passivity, our God-given, first-world entitlement to retirement and free hip replacements. I need a tropical cruise to get away from it all. I need a beach and a convertible. My planet owes me.

After all, meditation is just a few moments of not thinking. Repose of silence. An awareness with nothing more than the sound of the blood rushing in and out of your heart pump.

What could be gained by listening to your heart?

I don't know. My heart is so puny, so unbelievably unexercised as an organ of awareness, that meditation works on me like a Brita filter on an Alaskan oil spill. I close my eyes and the dark waters rush in, overwhelming me with thoughts of last days.

Last days.

Some people say the Earth is angry. Others speak of signs. I don't blame people for thinking this. On September 11th, 2001, when the twin towers were hit, I sped home and hugged my family and prayed that it would be over quick.

(In your home emergency kit, should you have a three-day supply of food and water or a twelve gauge and three boxes of shells or three cases of the softest toilet paper money can buy?)

Meditation is not exactly like prayer. It's not a wish. It's a connectedness to your core. It's listening through your mind into your body, down through your feet into the ground, into the soil, into the Earth's core, and down into the very essence of the planetary universe where sub-atomic particles are charged by the attraction called love.

My awareness from my brain bone to my shin bone to the bone of consciousness tells me one inexorable thing: we don't have much time to figure this stuff out.

Time is the trickiest bastard in the universe. That's why meditation is informed by a deep awareness of the tick tock. Tick tock. Human time is measured by an atomic clock, electrons swirling a neutron.

What is time but our awareness of our mortality? One day the heart beats no more. Evolution, whether you believe in it or not, tells us that individual lives are less important than the progression of the species. We live as long as we can pass the torch. We don't live for a thousand years. Death is a bright idea: individuals don't matter as much as the line, your line, your generational achievement.

What is our generational achievement?

My parents are gone. My grandparents, too. My children are my line. No, I am so wrong. Families do not exist, as races do not exist. There is only one human family.

That stranger across the world is your brother/sister for we exist together; everyone who exists in this continuum is a part of us. Our arc, this little curve of history, must be to achieve something bigger than our comfort.

Silence tells me that we are bound by our awareness of each other. Look at the scattered stars and the yellow moon. We exist together. We are trying to evolve. We must try to make things better. We must try to live with compassion and kindness. Today we must be kinder and more compassionate than yesterday.

Close your eyes – a mercenary in Tripoli reconsiders. Close your eyes – a woman dons a radiation suit in Fukushima. Close your eyes – and listen, not to your own heart, but to the pulse of the world community. Listen to the network of bonds that connect us to New Orleans, Kabul, Sendai, Benghazi, to life everywhere, to the distant forest smell of the newspaper that you hold in your hands, to the sorrow of your grandparent's enemies, and to the caress of the gentle wind that touches us all for all time.

Close your eyes. Sit quietly. And find us.

Thirsty for Fresh Knowledge of Our Waters

Canada has 20 percent of the world's fresh water, and the world's mind is thirsty.

My friend Codie, a senior executive, just had a baby. She also happens to live on a reserve ten minutes outside a small Canadian city.

Codie's baby boy is being raised on bottled water. Codie says she's used to cooking and brushing her teeth with bottled water. The river she lives beside is too polluted to drink. Thanks to decades of mining and agriculture, the fish are not safe to eat either.

Super Natural BC and not a drop to drink.

My friend Codie and many other people living on reserves have been drinking bottled water for decades. Clean water is the basis of life. The United Nations argue that water is a fundamental human right:

> "The human right to water entitles everyone to sufficient, safe, acceptable, physically accessible and affordable water for personal and domestic uses."
> *UN CESC - General Comment 15, para.2*

Maybe we should stop taking our water for granted. We

shouldn't do this just because our communities, wildlife, and agriculture depend upon it, but because Canada has a very special responsibility to lead when it comes to water.

It isn't our just our birthright, it is our global endowment.

Californians are screaming about the lack of water. Agriculture nearly everywhere is suffering. Closer to home, the sockeye fishery has just been closed. Water levels are disastrously low.

Okanagan Lake is a treasured legacy. Without it there would be no wine, no tourism, no Kelowna. The California drought should give everyone a reason to reflect. What should we do about protecting the health of our waterways?

Rather than point fingers or give up, we must clarify our mindset toward water. The Thames River in England was used for centuries as a sewer. The Los Angeles River was a garbage dump. Many of the world's greatest rivers barely make it to the ocean now.

The Citarum in Indonesia is so chocked full with mercury, arsenic, lead, and waste, it is the colour of crap. Four billion tons of waste go into China's Yellow River every year.

Okanagan Lake contains estrogen and other pharmaceuticals. Every pill we pop gets flushed in our waters. The consequences? We don't know. Science is barely catching up to the health impacts of drinking this chemical cocktail, but studies tell us that estrogen changes the gender of fish.

What happened? We are still stuck in old paradigms when it comes to water. We think chemicals and technology will be the answer. We convinced ourselves that dilution was the solution. If dilution didn't work, then surely technology would save the day.

Technology will not restore our streams, creeks, rivers, lakes, and oceans. Dams, channelization, invasive vegetation, pollution –

the impacts are systemic, so surely our solution must be systemic.

But we haven't put our minds to the big picture. The waters of the world are critical, but there is no current assessment of the health of our waterways. Who will be the stewards of our most precious legacy? Whose responsibility is the water when it crosses provincial and national boundaries?

Whose responsibility is it when decades of mineral exploitation, agriculture, and habitat damage come home to roost in the quality of our drinking water?

Is there anyone considering the total impact upon lives, habitat, and wildlife?

Look around you. Wetlands have disappeared. Companies have walked away from their responsibilities. Investments in sophisticated water quality testing have not kept up.

World class water quality is achieved by understanding that water quality is only as good as the weakest link in the chain. Habitat for diverse flora and fauna are essential, not just for their own sake, but as part of the water ecosystem.

Wetlands are not just for the birds, frogs, insects, and domestic cats. They create the necessary filtration needed to protect our water and create buffer zones to protect us from floods as well as regulate soil and nutrient retention.

The humble cattail, for example, has the power to filter run off. This reduces excess nutrients that can enter a water system. Cattails can prevent soil erosion. They also provide important habitat for wildlife and birds.

The lowly cattail is an example of the power of nature, beautifully filtering out massive amounts of nitrogen and phosphorous along with other pollutants with its own built-in genius.

Our thinking about water has been arrogant. We think we can fix it all later.

Instead, our minds must rise to the genius of nature. Science, biology, chemistry, and engineering are revealing that it is cleaner, cheaper, and healthier to utilize the wisdom of how nature *thinks*. Clean water is a product of the mind of nature.

Gregory Bateson offers a useful thought on a clean and healthy water system: "The major problems in the world are the result of the difference between how nature works and the way people think."

Who are the people who know how to think like nature?

I'll give you a hint. Fifty per cent of their reserves do not have safe drinking water in our province.

People like my friend Codie have profound hope. She knows that indigenous peoples, no matter how they have suffered, consider the water and land their sacred responsibility.

Let us listen to our indigenous friends and be thirsty for another way to be.

An Idiot's Guide to BC Politics and Economy

The conventional way we talk about politics is left wing vs. right wing. The left wing is supposed to consider people and the protection of people as a top priority. The right wing is supposed to consider jobs and the protection of the economy as a top priority.

A good left government protects you from capitalism. It helps you keep your job by supporting policies that favour your rights as a worker. Lefties, in general, care about human rights, economic equality, and social justice.

The left wing loves talking community, collective responsibility, and helping others. On the other hand, the right talks about individual responsibility, equality of opportunity, and the value of hard work.

A good right government protects you from socialism. It helps you keep your job by creating a competitive situation for your employer such as low taxes, minimal regulations, and self-reliance.

A job, the right says, is the best social program.

In BC, the usual left vs. right thinking is considered old school. Too simplistic. We, the people of BC, prefer a balanced approach. Some notice the contradictions in this approach. Maybe we are both?

In BC, we love our health care. Medicare was invented by a left winger, but even right wingers know that our system, while expensive, is one of the keys to a society that is strong enough to compete on the world stage.

In BC, we love our environment. Left wingers love it so much that they would sacrifice a wee bit of wealth for it. Right wingers love it so much they abandon their home provinces to retire to the Okanagan where they can enjoy an environment unspoiled by industry.

In BC, we have our differences, but we also have things that unite us. Like we hate high taxes. Left and right are united in believing government is too big, even though in BC we have less government per one thousand people than every other province, according to policyalternatives.ca.

Left wingers want corporations to pay more taxes. Right wingers want to keep taxes low so they can keep more money, invest, and attract businesses. Both groups share a belief that a balanced approach toward taxes is a good thing.

Turns out that left wingers like jobs, too.

But right and left wingers hate poverty. Artistic lefties hate it so much they will buy houses in run down areas and work hard to make them nice so they can sell them to righties who will flip them to each other.

Both groups volunteer at non-profits and give money to charities. It is a known fact that low income people give away a bigger share of their income than wealthier folks.

On Sundays, both groups attend church or bingo, but left wing churches are going out of business compared to evangelical churches. Some right wingers behave as if JC was a capitalist, not a left wing radical who scared the bejesus out of the establishment.

On the other days of the week, left and right wingers watch too much TV, eat too much junk food, and cheat on their spouses in fairly equal numbers.

Low income citizens often vote right even when this would negatively impact their job security and slim wallets. A US example? Obama is not very popular with low income white people even though he has brought them health care.

On the other hand, rich or well-to-do people, in general, vote right (even those that went to university and took sociology).

Rich people don't love their taxes going to people who are lazy. And in general, lazy is a code word for people who are different. Not everybody likes to give their attention to people who think differently. Take note aboriginals, disabled folks, and federal scientists.

What about left wingers? Left wingers possess post-secondary achievement at levels that are above the norm, so that's why they prefer self-interested causes like parks, bike lanes, and community gardens.

In fact, the Greens accuse the NDP of abandoning the environment in favour of jobs. In the words of Kermit, it's not easy being green.

Lefties of all colours went bonkers recently because the NDP formed the provincial government in Alberta. This crazy seesawing usually happens only in BC, eh? Experts say that voter frustration, not political allegiance impacted the *orange crush*.

But even with all this excitement, many consider politics boring or even irrelevant. How could someone say our political and economic destiny is irrelevant?

Well, they simply point to the influence of US trade and multinational corporations. They point to Hongcouver's real estate being controlled by Chinese money. They point to our economic lives being controlled by entities outside the province.

Smart people question whether any elected government can effect anything more than minor change. So what do we do?

No matter if you are left or right, orange or green, it might be important to a democratic country to be able to control our air, water, and land. After all, doesn't our health and prosperity depend upon the strength of our democracy?

Democracy is about the freedom to choose to be left wing or right wing or both, not the freedom to make meaningful choice impossible.

And, in the end, we must ask what they're asking in Greece, the birthplace of democracy: what is the purpose of freedom? What is the purpose of a democracy, an economy, a community . . . of life?

A Rare and Beautiful Authority

One autumn day, many years ago, I went from being a worker to a manager. One second I was the servant, the next, the boss. Be careful. It may happen to you.

The transition from employee to employer is fun at first. Whew, you get to drive the bus. You get to wander back stage where the budgets and perks are kept. You look in the mirror, and you say you're going to be a great leader, the kind of boss you always wanted to have.

Then, one day, someone shows you a survey. According to the survey, you're a great guy and well, a pretty average leader.

At first you blame it on others. It's your employees who are simply blaming you for their incompetence. Geez, they can't accept your authority ever since you've been promoted/elected.

You know things now, you reason, and that's why they can't accept you. Like what is inside the file at HR. Like who is on medication. Who is unable and who is strong.

When you become a boss, you also find out a little about yourself. That you really like being liked. That praise is juicy. That you're entitled to those perks. And one other thing . . . that power can corrupt.

The difference between the average leader and the great one is not obvious. In all the scholarship around management, experts have found no scientific way to measure management effectiveness. Even in sports, which is generally obsessed with statistical measurement, we can't find the secret, the one thing.

Look at our fascination with sports dynasties and companies like Apple. We are obsessed with Steve Jobs because we want to enter that promised land of exceptional leadership.

The most important thing we can learn from Jobs is the fact that great management is not a gift. Leadership greatness, it turns out, is not about intuition, creativity, or flashes of brilliance. Nor is it about style, charisma, or intimidation.

Here's a hint. Great leadership is linked to informed and disciplined practice accomplished over many years. Practice? What kind of practice?

Great leaders do not practice obedience, but rather they practice respectful disobedience in order to deliver value, innovation, and differentiation. The last thing Steve Jobs wanted to hear was something like, "Hey, we've always done it this way."

Great leaders practice questioning their assumptions, not pledging blind obedience to anyone or anything.

Great leaders practice inspiring others to question even their own authority. Like great parents, great leaders teach us not dependence, but independence. Great leaders help set us free to be the best version of ourselves. (How often do you practice that?)

We know that disobedience and questioning are frightening things to practice for the average person. It's so much easier to relax and do what everyone else does. But without a little disobedience, what in the world would actually change?

Yes, we must know when to respect the rules, but we must also know when they must be broken. We must know when to follow the path and when to strike out for a new one.

Are you the kind of boss that inspires a little disobedience? Or do you clamp down on it because it makes you feel a loss of control? Do you inspire greatness or do you strike fear?

The new science of expertise tells us that in order to be really good at anything you need to practice. If you want to be great at anything, you need 10,000 hours of informed practice.

How much practice did I have before I became a boss? How much practice did I have in successfully inspiring people to challenge my authority, break the unbreakable, and engender independent thought? Not much, I'm afraid.

The practice of great leadership requires managers to constantly practice asking questions, defy conventional thinking, and challenge patterns of thought. The best practice for leadership may be to teach those above you to value dissent.

This may sound illogical and crazy, but there is nothing more dangerous than a boss who is afraid to defy his own boss. If you socialize yourself to respect authority too much, you'll develop little tolerance for critical questioning. Middle management is filled with mini-Napoleons convinced that sucking up or relationship development will deliver the results.

I've seen Napoleon in my bathroom mirror and the hat fit a little too well. My mirror says that inside every expert suck up, there is also an insecure bully.

How do you know you've become the boss from hell? Easy, the boss from hell won't do one very simple human act: admit failure and apologize.

Olympic gold medal winners teach us that failure is a critical part of success, especially when it is the kind of failure that reveals the

Napoleon-from-within, the insecure soul filled with ego-blindness and a great desire to control others.

Do you have a great boss? Are you a great boss? When is the last time your boss demonstrated humility? When is the last time you said to someone who reports to you, "I'm sorry."

Great leadership is a function of practicing two things over and over again: unfailing personal humility; and the courage to be openly honest. If you analyze humility and honesty, you will find that they have everything to do with a rare and beautiful kind of authority, a quality we find in our greatest leaders.

Not the kind of authority that comes with power and threat, but the kind of authority that is freely given to you, that is offered to you as a sign of faith, trust, and hope.

Who the Heck Are You? Relationship-Centred Leadership

Now that I have been a boss for a long time and made nearly every mistake a person can make, and hurt a lot of people, and climbed a lot of mountains with others, I will tell you what I have learned.

A friend who has been working for a university president had this to say about him: "I've worked my tail off for three years. Not once has he asked me a question about me. He doesn't even see me."

I have another friend who would do anything for his boss. This is what he has to say: "Sometimes I think my boss knows me better than I know myself. She gives me a chance to rethink what I need to rethink. She trusts me, but also knows when I need a gentle push. She asks me about my life before she talks business. I believe she really knows me as a person."

Sometimes people are pretty darn uncomfortable knowing anything personal about a colleague. They worry about not being able to be objective. They fret about being manipulated. Ain't none of your business, they say.

Here's what my boss says: "I practice relationship-centred leadership. We work in a people enterprise. How can we ask people to care, if we don't value relationships? Every moment of interaction is an opportunity to deepen a relationship, to make it more trusting, to confirm values, to co-create a brighter future, to inspire each other."

Is relationship-centred leadership just another flavour of the month? Are we talking about yucky friendship here? Are we talking about crossing the line into areas of personal privacy?

Here is what an HR expert says: "We don't need to know every personal detail, but human beings are human beings. We are all walking a journey. When that journey gets tough, we need to let our employees know they are not alone. We are here to be supportive. We are on this journey together."

Others are a little bit crass about all this caring. "The more you care," says one colleague, "the more productive that employee will be."

Hold on, you say. Maybe the employer doesn't have the right to know your personal details. This is all a dark ploy to get deeper engagement and more productivity. All of this is about just one thing: money.

Interesting point, says a friend who is currently the vice-president of a multi-national organization. "What is wrong with treating people right *and* making money? Don't the two go hand in hand?"

Ask a teacher. Do teachers believe it is important to know the student? Do they believe that understanding who the student is, where he/she comes from, how much he/she knows is important? Or do you prefer a teacher who couldn't care less who you are, where you come from, or what you already know?

I once had a boss who only pretended to care. He told people what they wanted to hear. He shook a lot of hands and he smiled a lot. People who didn't really know him thought he was pretty effective, too.

He's retired now. I recently asked him if he had any regrets. This is what he said: "I don't go out as much now because in my heart I don't want to run across people from my old role. I didn't put enough heart and soul into defending people, supporting people, working on behalf of their souls."

I could not believe he said souls. But he wanted me to know that being a good boss is a kind of soul craft. In relationship-centred leadership, people matter most. The work is not what you typically think. The work IS the relationship.

The equation is simple. If the relationship is excellent, the work is excellent. If the relationship is weak, the work is weak.

More threats, the more impossible deadlines, the more ultimatums, the more of this you do – the worse it almost always gets.

The more trust, the more effort on having difficult conversations, the more caring, the more honesty, the more you strengthen the relationships at work – the easier the heavy lifting becomes.

And the more delightful. The more like soul craft. The more valuable the work becomes, the more spiritual it becomes and the more connected to a better a way of living.

Relationships do require a lot of listening, a ton of exploring, and many miscues and mistakes. But the end result is a stronger partnership, an enlightened relationship, one that can withstand the dehumanizing forces of the global economy.

What is true at work is also true in families. Families, like workplaces, are torn apart by command and control bullies. Families and workplaces can be poisoned by silence, people giving up on each other, and the quiet steady erosion of trust.

So how do we begin?

The basic building block of any relationship is interest in the Other. Not feigned interest. Not pretend caring, but genuine interest in another soul.

"I've worked with you for three years," my friend finally asked, "why is it that you've never asked me a question about myself or my family?"

The boss stood there dumbfounded. There was a long pause. There was a moment of great discomfort.

"Well, I don't know," he said. "Let me tell you that I am kind of pleased you asked. That took courage to say. I've been so busy and so focussed, but that is no excuse. Let me ask you this. Can we start again?"

"Start again?"

"Did you know that you are one of our most valuable people? I have been so remiss. If you don't mind me asking, who the heck are you?"

The Wild
Versus
The Park

Like a manicured golf course, my life is a domesticated and safe wonderland where the world is a park – fun, safe, and controlled. And like any park, it is hard to know who made it, who controls it, and why we can't leave.

Few people know how to enter The Wild, yet we need it so much.

The Wild is a place nobody goes anymore. We have domesticated our lives inside and outside. Our routines are contained in a beautiful and undisturbed golf course. We toss back drinks, but our beds are burning.

I don't even remember what it was like not to be controlled. I work, sleep, eat, and watch TV. I am programmed to achieve career goals and retire. I really don't know what lies beyond the fence.

Is this all there is to life in The Park?

We all feel the push for ownership. We take part in lives of comparison. We put our children on the treadmill, the racetrack, the exhibition of skills, whatever you want to call it, so that they can eagerly line up and follow the path. What's wrong with a domesticated life?

Other countries seem farther ahead than us. One country advertises a completely indoor life. You never have to step outside. Another has citizens who have grown uncomfortable with gardening, with sitting outside, so their worlds commence entirely in front of their TV, computer, and handheld screens.

The Wild. It's a dangerous place, that's why nobody wants to go there. Why would we want to enter The Wild anyway?

There are other nations who remember The Wild. They still glorify, not just the outdoors, but the Wilderness in Our Hearts. First Nations, as they are called in Canada, partake in ceremonies that call forth The Wild.

Most of us have lost the rituals and celebrations that bring the human animal together with the living planet.

I have my wild moments when I am so happy I want to do uncivilized things such as embrace a stranger, swim toward the moon, or run with a spear toward prey. Our memories go back thousands of years.

I am running, you are there, too. We are Running For Our Lives.

The wild places in our hearts are really undiscovered places. They are the places of connection, sharing, and passion. They are also frightening in that they teach us how civilized we are, how out of touch, how lost.

I am lost. This keyboard is all I feel. The sun is shining somewhere, but not on my face, not warming my heart, not connecting with you, so that we can heal ourselves and escape this 24-hour amusement park.

Instead, we don't work for each other anymore. Corporations ask us to compete to have even more than we need. With technology and medicine, we are rich enough to take care of every single child. But at this park, we leave people behind, look down on the broken streets from our penthouses, and drive vehicles appropriately armoured from compassion.

The wild person walks alone in the wilderness to discover, first and foremost, the suffering that builds and nurtures civilization. What are we so afraid of?

In our dreams, the wild heart cries out for the knowledge of our ancestors. Most families park their ancestors in care homes so that their wisdom, medicated and managed by others, disappears into the wind.

The Wild connects us with our suffering. The Park tells us to watch TV. The Wild teaches us to distrust human-made things. The Park tells us to learn, earn, and retire.

Last night I dreamed you were with me. All our possessions were gone. The world was on fire. We mourned the polluted lake and genetically altered plants and animals. We looked up at the sun, knowing that we were lost, that perhaps beyond the walls of the amusement park, we could find the freedom to be ourselves.

I still remember the fear.

In our dream, we found the secret door and saw the machinery behind everything we believed was real. We knew and understood we had to find The Wild, which wasn't the name of an actual place at all.

I asked you what The Wild was and you looked at me and you began to shimmer. I watched you vibrate, and I heard a faint humming sound and saw that you were vibrating as if you were an image projected on a monitor.

And I saw you as a projection, an image created by us, the

captive owners of the amusement park. In my dream, we were ghosts, barely alive, animated only by our life support, the poisoned food we design and manufacture.

How do we come alive? How do we feel? How do we awaken? How do we face the truth of our lives and world?

Because of the dream, I left nearly everything and realized that even though it was too late for me, we could do something.

We asked our children what would happen if we took them away from the amusement park, away from the fenced backyard, away from the playgrounds, away from the grid of desks at school.

What would happen if we wanted to be wild, we asked.

Where would we go? They asked. How would we be? How would we live?

I don't know, I said. I don't know.

Hot Breath

of Tiger

Be still. What my grandmother told me about tigers stays with me. In Korea, where I grew up, there used to be a lot of tigers, which, of course, have been extinct for many decades. My grandmother told me that a tiger could call out to you in a human voice.

Tigers, she would say, especially late at night, were not like other animals. They hunted you.

There is a saying that goes like this: Six months of the year Koreans hunt tigers – the other six months of the year, the tigers hunt Koreans.

After running off with your livestock, the Korean Siberian tiger would stalk you and kill you in a manner I will simply describe as supernatural.

And in the stories my grandmother used to tell us, I always got the feeling the natural world was unified somehow, that one day, if I didn't behave properly, I'd be woken up during the night with the hot breath of a tiger on my face.

Western literature is filled with tigers. From the poet Blake and Kipling's Jungle Book to recently acclaimed books by John Vaillant and Tea Obreht. Tigers are hauntingly evocative creatures.

When I was a small boy, I lived in the city of Seoul. South Korea in the 50s and 60s was essentially an agrarian society moving toward industrialization. A country of peasants and artists who lived under Japanese occupation for many decades.

Koreans are a proud people. We are proud of our culture and proud of our secrets.

I remember my grandmother's outhouse. I remember balancing on a thick branch and using old newspapers. Yes, and down there. Pigs.

We lived in an old two-story house made of concrete cinders. We slept in the main room on layers of bedding spread out on the cold floor. At night, Grandmother, who was an illiterate Baptist Christian, told us stories while we listened to the wind.

We were very afraid at night. Seoul was a city recovering from a devastating war. There were many thieves. Pick-pockets with razors to slit the bottoms of your pockets. Everywhere.

And tigers, too. To steal children from their beds. To punish evil. To avenge the future.

During the day, the streets were busy. My grandmother rented the room below us. We ate rice with hot water, vegetables, and pickled cabbage. Sometimes we enjoyed ox tail soup or boiled pork with our round metal spoons and wood chopsticks.

Merchants came from the countryside to sell fruits and vegetables at the market. I asked my grandmother to carry me, but I was getting too big. She let go of my hand and I followed her long skirt.

The world was not big and bright and natural. Instead, it was gray, filled with asphalt, dust, and smoke. Bus exhaust fouled the air. Nobody noticed me. I watched a plane fly overhead. I followed it until it disappeared into the silver sky.

When I looked for my grandmother, I knew I might be lost. But I didn't care, even though I had been trained by humans to be afraid.

124

I wandered around the market. Only decades before, you could find luxurious tiger pelts in these markets. Did you know that winter is the best time for hunting tiger?

Tiger fur is very warm and especially thick in the winter. Footprints in snow, some as wide as a man's hands outspread, helped with tracking them.

There are stories about tigers breaking into houses and stealing children. There are stories about tigers attacking horses. The Japanese rulers prevented Koreans from carrying firearms, so people in the villages made traps for them. Dogs were often used as bait.

There are two stories about tigers. One is a creation myth based on the idea that the Korean mountainside looks just like a tiger. The mountains are steep and very rounded at the top. When the mist rolls in layers, the land resembles a tiger.

The other story is that Koreans cut down all the trees because of the great fear of tigers. Today, there are no tigers or old trees in my home country.

When I realized I couldn't find my way back to grandmother's house, I wanted to cry but I walked around until I found a young policeman.

"Where do you live, little boy?"

"I live with my grandmother and sister."

"Where are your parents?"

"I don't have parents. They went to a place called Canada."

"If you tell me your grandmother's name, I will take you home."

When I got home, my grandmother hugged me and cried out in relief. She told me how afraid she had been. She had prayed to Jesus. Later, after the policeman had left, she hit my legs many times with a thin reed.

That night I dreamed for a tiger to come to our house. I prayed I might become a tiger and possess two abilities. To be feared and powerful and to wander wherever I pleased.

Now I am old. When I think of tigers, I feel something within me from the days so long ago. Nearly everything about me is human but some very tiny part of me may be part tiger.

And that part of me, the part that contains instinct, tells me one overwhelming thing: protect your family and run. But there is no place to run. And the trees are gone. And the people surround us.

For the People: Fire, Sumac and Ethan Baptiste

Editor's note: Ethan Baptiste died on June 8th 2010

"I still believe that Council should be measured by
their impact on the community. That means, in two
years, membership should ask: Has the drugs and
alcohol problem gotten better or worse? Have more
kids dropped out of high school, or less? How many
of our members were sent to jail? How many members
get diabetes or other health problems? How many
students finished college/university?"
Ethan Baptiste

The Inkameep Indian Reserve, on the outskirts of Oliver, sits in a
low arid valley. In the distance stands McIntyre Bluff, known in the
Okanagan language as snqilt. The high cliffs appear after you pass
Vaseux Lake, and they tower above the highway so much so that
you feel kind of squeezed.

It is Saturday and my friend Ann and I pull off to the side of the road. Road dust fills my nose. We can't park anywhere near the address because vehicles are parked everywhere. We squeeze between two trucks and step out. We follow a man in braids wearing Wranglers.

"I feel sick inside," Ann says quietly. I know what she means.

"Me, too," I say. I'm glad she's here. Our friend meant a lot to us, but we can see we are not alone.

On a reserve like this you won't find fancy homes. Ethan's childhood home is a small one-story bungalow. Tall ponderosa pines stand in the north. One of my favourite indigenous trees, the sumac, surrounds the front lawn.

Christmas lights hang along the eaves. The house is well kept; it is dark green. We step across cactus and stand under a wide mountain ash. The shade is cool. People huddle everywhere. A young girl hugs an older man.

The sky is broad and blue. A white tent has been set up with rows of chairs beneath. Elders sit quietly. We find a spot in front of the kitchen window. There isn't enough room in the house, so the family has set up speakers. There are two portable washrooms, too.

A short man with ropey wrists and black hair quietly hands out bottles of water. Since the news of the accident, I am surprised to find tears in my eyes when I least expect it. I don't cry very much. I want to, but I never do.

A man tends a huge bonfire. (The fire is lit as soon as the news reaches the family that a death has occurred, and it will remain lit until sundown of the day of the burial.) He wears a special light blue bandana given by the family. The fire burns hot and clean. Waves ripple upward and disappear.

Ann has her arms crossed. Behind her sunglasses, it's tough to know what she's feeling. She and Leif worked with Ethan on the college's environmental diplomas. I start counting people. I lose track at five hundred. I look for my friend James. I see Donna, Robert, and Francie.

The kitchen window opens, but I can't see the person speaking. I can hear her voice. It is strong and clean and clear like the sky. But the voice cracks over the loudspeaker. In the south, near the horizon, there is one cloud.

The drummers are called into the house. Six or seven men make their way through all the people and enter the house on the side.

"We thank the Creator for Ethan," the female voice says. "We thank the Creator for giving us Ethan, and now he is with the Creator again."

I am surprised by the Elders who speak because even though we are in pain, these people do not lead with their individual pain as westerners might. They lead with thanks, with gratitude.

I cannot understand the depth of their grief; nor can I fully understand their resolute strength.

I know there are many who have not worked, celebrated, and learned with aboriginal people. I have been very fortunate to have some experience. What I know is this: in all areas of inquiry, from social work to medicine, to biology and poetry, indigenous knowledge and practice are at the forefront of human innovation and discovery.

"We are so grateful to Ethan's parents for raising him," another Elder says.

This celebration of his life is unexpected for me. Even though Ethan taught at Okanagan College, worked as an aboriginal mentor, studied at UBC, and spoke to me and my colleagues often, I realize at this moment that despite all that you hear about aboriginal culture, there is so much we can learn and so much that is a mystery.

Ethan used his smile, advanced degrees, and knowledge of traditional ways, to serve his community. At the age of 33, he was a role model. Ethan's pursuits captivated me. His pursuit of the PhD, pursuit of the leadership of the Osoyoos Band, and his pursuit of a larger understanding of economic and social development for his people within an indigenous framework – these things gave me and so many others great inspiration.

"People from everywhere are here," Ann says. Ethan's ancestry points to a time when great chiefs from near and far attempted to collaborate around shared issues and goals.

Another Elder takes the microphone and makes us all laugh. "Sometimes we got to see things in a lighter way," he says. "I remember what Ethan said when he wasn't sure, 'we're doing it for the people,' he said.

There is drumming and there is song and there are women's voices at the microphone. I am glad I am wearing sunglasses because I cannot stop my eyes. Ethan, we all realize, was a rare and special leader with a grassroots base, a superb education, and a vision of social justice.

He would talk about hunting, going to powwows, and the need for more thinkers like the valley's own great Syilx writer, activist, and scholar, Jeannette Armstrong.

Since I was a child, I have always secretly wished that I were First Nations. Maybe it was because I was tired of being teased. Maybe it was because of my youthful identification with stereotypical heroes like Tonto. Maybe it was because my Indian friends, like Vincent

Joe, knew how to handle themselves.

"Who do you want to be?" Vincent used to say.

"Tonto," I said.

"I want to be Bruce Lee. Okay, grasshopper?"

When I was a kid in Williams Lake, Vincent used to drive me around town. We were both twelve.

Today, I admire indigenous intellectuals who provide alternative ways of thinking about our impossible problems. Our great and threatened indigenous cultures all over this planet have shown us many powerful ways of knowing, feeling, and experiencing.

Ethan's quiet smile and gentle, non-confrontational way transformed his students. They began to see, respect, and strive to understand how our own traditions have been constructed by colonial ideas and practices. His PhD examined a Syilx way of economic development.

One of the first ways to appreciate another person's culture is to delve into your own. There are many people who identify themselves as white, but do not understand how their own ethnicity has been forgotten or even erased.

People ask me why I can't speak Korean. They are surprised when I tell them I was not allowed to speak it. My parents thought I needed English.

What makes us different can so easily be lost.

Ethan said, "Protect the land, protect the people."

There is a long line up to go into Ernest and Maxine's house. The hot desert sun makes Oliver the wine capital of Canada. It is also home to one of the richest, most diverse, and most endangered ecological areas on this continent. It is also the home of a proud First Nations people who honour us and themselves by protecting their language, culture, and identity.

It is also the home of Ethan Baptiste.

Thank you to Maxine Baptiste
who gave me permission to write this about her son.

Click, Click, Boom: The Secrets of Dark Innovation

Economists argue we inhabit a new zone where the information economy is becoming the innovation economy. Innovation is the new economic and political reality. Bank presidents, farmers, gamers, and politicians agree this is *the* hot zone.

If innovation is the new global currency, then what is *dark innovation*?

Dark innovation is new stuff designed to hurt people and the planet. For example, military leaders describe the new soldier, one that fights in the so-called dark Internet using tools seen in science fiction.

In a time when disabling a country's Internet means crippling the country's economy, we are investing in technologies that will disrupt banking systems, track and freeze assets wherever they exist, and level the economic playing field with a variety of Internet attacks.

This is not grandpa's science fiction: Someday all wars will be waged in cyberspace.

Dark innovation used to refer to the thinking that enabled military innovation. These were new weapons, smart ways to kill or disable, including non-lethal biological warfare. But we've moved beyond the products of creative weaponry. Dark innovation also refers to a set of tools used to fight innovation itself and its own ideological march to progress. Dark innovation, then, is also a strike against innovation as conceived by global capitalism.

Dark innovators don't automatically assume that innovation refers to products and services. Does product innovation always lead to well-being? Some, like Edward Snowden, support the kind of innovation that will destabilize the mechanisms of government sanctioned cyber-espionage, invasions against sovereignty, and perhaps more.

Forget about dark innovation as the gimmicks of James Bond. Here is the core destabilizing question: What kind of innovation leads to true well-being and human emancipation? What kind of innovation would set us free?

Unlike the conventional entrepreneur, dark innovators don't assume that innovation should be about exports, helping one country defeat another in a trade war. In fact, innovators who unconsciously use the win/lose paradigm are not true innovators in my book because they don't see how trapped we are in the very economic paradigm that created us.

Dark innovators agree that we live in an innovation economy. They point out that innovation in the hands of the powerful will always serve their needs.

Can dark innovation be a tool that empowers the disempowered? Can it help the taxpayer extract more value from the bureaucracy?

In my view, dark innovation represents the art of thinking differently about the negative aspects of how new ideas make us think, feel, and behave. At no other time in human history are there fewer alternative ways of life, fewer sources of non-violent rebellion, and fewer sources of credible social economic and political critique.

How do we wage battle with a global market where 1% owns nearly 90%? In our current economic regime, will the poor merely get poorer and rich get richer? Is that the human trajectory of this global economy? Dark innovators helped create Naomi Klein's version of disaster capitalism. We saw in successive Middle East conflicts that war actually lined the pockets of multinational corporations as governments outsourced everything from weapons, food, security, and first world lives.

For the young people of the Middle East disaster capitalism has meant billions of dollars of revenue for the defence industry and all its partners. Even in North America, oil cleanup and environment restoration is big business.

Some dark innovators have turned their attention to using social media to manipulate public opinion. Social media elects governments and tears them down. But who controls social media? The art of the click (click bait as they say) has reached epic proportions in the war for your attention as a new breed of media companies demonstrate their effectiveness in herding millions of clicks.

Click. Click. Boom.

Dark innovators know how to use Facebook to assess, shape, and drive public opinion. We see it every day in what we call the news. News programs compete for clicks like everyone else. There is nothing like a disaster, war, or a scandal to drive up ratings, advertising, and credibility.

Dark innovators also know that social media has a huge potential to create unexpected social and economic change. Twitter and Facebook have saved lives in emergencies. An unknown Obama would have never been elected without social media. Many people are using platforms like eBay and VRBO to make an independent living without reporting to a boss.

Innovation can chain us or set us free. But it is not product innovation that we need. It is, probably, innovation around the thorniest of our problems: human nature. Will the problems of inequality, violence, and environmental disaster be addressed by a product or a device?

Will childhood violence and poverty during the richest point in human history be solved by the Internet? Dark innovation, as expressed by the human genome, artificial intelligence, and nanotechnology may be half the way there.

Three Developments to Watch

1. A most interesting development is machine-assisted human augmentation. Not only will computers drive your car, but computers will be going dark: reducing crime, personalizing training, creating weather, and in general, saving us from each other.

2. Another development of dark innovators is introducing more chaos into the systems to keep them healthy. Adding chaos into systems allows these smart systems to prepare for errors, anomalies, and intrusions. A system like Netflix uses computer agents to attempt to disrupt the system. This allows the system to learn to adjust to all manner of events, eventually making any sort of failure a non-event.

3. Finally, dark innovators are interested in solving problems

within the context of late stage capitalism. Through the use of big data, scientists at MIT are discovering the economic value of egalitarian social environments. Researchers are suggesting there is a formula emerging for human well-being and productivity at work that does not remotely look like the cubicle farms and hierarchical towers of today.

Will dark innovation destroy the planet, help us live in peace, or will it create more Facebook game requests? Stay tuned.

Leading from the Future as it Emerges: Soul Change

The phrase, *paradigm shift*, is probably familiar to you. Coined by Thomas Kuhn, the phrase has reached cliché status. A similar phrase is, *think outside the box*. Most of us know what people are striving for when they use such phrases.

For example, those who are concerned about healthcare often call for *disruptive innovation* in health care management. Disruptive innovation happens all the time in the technology market, according to Harvard professor Clayton Christensen. He introduced the term to describe everything from how digital disrupted film, computer printers disrupted offset printing, steamships disrupted sailing ships, telephone to telegraphy, and so on.

What we need now, according to many health care experts, is something to disrupt the rising costs of health care. Others point to the electric car industry as potentially disrupting the oil industry. Not a minute too soon, many of us cry, as the planet is choking.

Still others say we should focus on the thinking that has caused us to despoil our planet and so cruelly hurt each other.

But won't technology save us? As much as we wax our hybrids, delight in YouTube, and pinch our iPhones, the last thing we can count on is technology to come and save day.

Technology will not stop people from getting cancer. Science won't tell us how to stop war. This is not to say that technology isn't useful, but where will we find a technology for our souls, our spirit, and our essence as human beings?

And if we really want to confront ourselves, we should remind ourselves of what Einstein said: "Problems cannot be solved at the same level of thinking that created them."

Spiritual researchers, religious thinkers, poets, and artists tell us that it seems as though thinking itself is the problem. We should feel more and think less, some say. But we've been hearing this stuff since day one and where has it gotten us?

Others say that if we want a huge paradigm shift, it ought to happen in our consciousness or awareness. We need a new way of being. We don't need newer buildings, faster Internet, or more tax cuts. We need a new way of responding to the world.

Easy to say, hard to do. But in many academic, business, cultural, and social leadership circles today, this new kind of being is being discussed as a potential paradigm shift, as a possible way of disrupting our very souls.

Psychologists Bishop et al. (2004) describe mindfulness as a two part operation:

> "The first component involves the self-regulation of attention so that it is maintained on immediate experience, thereby allowing for increased recognition of mental events in the present moment. The second

component involves adopting a particular orientation toward one's experiences in the present moment, an orientation that is characterized by curiosity, openness, and acceptance."

Many would call this definition very close to meditation. You'd be right if you pointed to the influence of Buddhism. You'd also be right that there is a massive amount of research going into, not just the therapeutic benefits of mindfulness, but into why mindfulness may be one of the ways we break the paradigm and save ourselves from ourselves.

The ability to experience your thoughts, control your concentration, and perhaps direct your thinking beyond its own boundaries is of great interest to intelligent people. Their basic question is this: what it would take to heal this world, stop the nonsense, and bring us into alignment with peace, compassion, and genuine respect?

Yes, I know this kind of talk is nearly as ridiculous as sending someone to the moon or postulating a round instead of a flat planet. Can we really change human nature? Can becoming more present in a moment of time really be the answer?

All I can say is that there is absolutely nothing to lose by learning how to be more mindful, more aware, and more able to think in alternative ways.

Not convinced?

Today you'll see police forces training their officers to be mindful. Medical schools are training their doctors to be more mindful of themselves and their patients. Harvard Law School is teaching it. Mindfulness is being taught in prisons, and it's working. Even the US Army is into it. Therapists are using it to help people reduce stress, become healthier and happier. Olympic athletes depend upon it.

There are good studies that show the benefits, but is it a game changer? Can it disrupt us? Will it take us to a better place?

The Presencing Institute, a most ambitious group of thought leaders, is "an awareness based action research community for profound societal innovation and change." It says on their website that "the presencing process is a journey that connects us more deeply both to what wants to emerge in the world and to our emerging, higher self."

Even loyal readers will have to read that quotation twice. To sum up, what this very potent group of thinkers have to say isn't particularly easy, but I'm going to give it shot.

These people believe the way you perceive a situation dictates how that situation will unfold. In other words, if we want a different kind of future, we have to perceive things differently, now, right NOW.

We have to see differently. Smell differently. Think differently. We have to use our senses, our bodies, and our connected minds to initiate a new level of mindfulness, one that is deeply transformation and co-creative.

Meditate the change.

One of the important scholars at the heart of this movement is Peter Senge, a pioneering organizational thinker and author of the landmark book *Fifth Discipline*.

One of the keys to their argument is our own inability to see our blind spots. Because of blind spots, we cannot see where we need to go. We keep repeating our mistakes. We raise our children no differently. Despite our great discoveries, our immense computing power, our unbelievable wealth, we have failed to rise to our higher selves.

Like you, I often think about what kind of change is needed in the world. I write about my own journey so that I can better understand my own blind spots. In many ways, the Presencing Institute is an example of the most forward kind of research on the planet.

Those who practice mindfulness give me hope that we can solve our problems without creating worse ones. I have hope that by exploring ourselves, we can discover a path to unfettered compassion, to understanding how to create soul change.

In the most simplistic terms, we must learn to become more open. More open to possibility. More open to ourselves. More open to forgiveness and reconciliation. And finally more open to a new way of being.

The 7 Practices
of Peaceful People

Ever meet a peaceful person? They are calm. They are cool. They are often very beautiful to have around. A peaceful person reacts with insight and generosity while the rest of us threaten to go thermonuclear.

A peaceful person can diffuse a challenging situation while the rest of us hire lawyers, plot revenge, and grin through our teeth. It is not easy to be peaceful, especially when we go to battle with our partners, our communities, our government, and our culture. In times of recession, the peaceful person has the presence of mind to generate solutions while everyone else is frozen by self-interest, fear, or panic.

Peaceful people, well, they advocate for global and local peace, but they also bring peace down to a microscopic level by making sure their hearts and minds are calm. What the peaceful know better than others is how to forgive the unforgivable.

Your forgiveness skills say a lot about your maturity.

Peaceful people have the skills to make a positive contribution to a world teeming with discord by focusing on each personal interaction as an opportunity to do one thing: listen. Listening is the peaceful person's core competency.

Here are seven strategies to finding more peace in your life.

7. Respect those not present

A peaceful person is never critical of someone when he or she is not in the room. Talking behind someone's back nearly always backfires. A peaceful person does not bad mouth others. Instead they consider what about another requires more value and appreciation. Be true to those who are not present by expressing how much you value someone who is not there, especially if they are your rival.

6. Acknowledge your feelings

A peaceful person expresses emotion as a way of recognizing the truth of his or her own heart. They are not afraid of emotion; nor does emotion rule the mind. By stating how you feel, you can acknowledge emotion and recognize it for what it is. Emotions are very important, but they do not represent the full picture. A peaceful person always acknowledges the power of emotion. An awareness of emotion allows us the ability to find peace in every situation. Once you state how you feel, you can step outside that emotion and behold it. This is what sadness feels like this morning, but in recognizing this, I am not sad anymore.

5. Help your body smile

A peaceful person is not just a feeler or a thinker. A peaceful person acknowledges the sacred power of the body. The body possesses a deep consciousness of its own. A smiling body is not difficult to achieve. It begins and ends with listening. It begins with nourishing sleep, regular exercise, and healing foods. The body smiles when it lives in harmony with its surroundings. Peace is easier to achieve when the environment is clean, the light natural, and noise levels soothing. Help your body smile by walking in the Sunday natural light after a long and restful sleep.

4. Seek warm-heartedness in times of conflict

Warm-heartedness is an approach to human interaction. Warm-heartedness brings peace because it recognizes difference and embraces uniqueness. Warm-heartedness can diffuse conflict by allowing conflict to express itself in terms of culture, situation, and history. Warm-heartedness allows empathy to build bridges, discover common points of gratitude, and melt differences. Be warm-hearted, it is the natural state of the peaceful person.

3. Practice communicating gratitude

Gratitude can break the spirit of anger and bitterness. Gratitude can flood the heart with forgiveness, especially when the past threatens to destroy us. Practicing gratitude is as easy as writing an email to yourself. What are you grateful for? I am grateful for the opportunity to take another breath as I type this. I am grateful for this beautiful day. Confront your rival with gratitude and see what happens.

2. Inspire your spirit by clearing your mind.

Clearing your mind allows you to separate your ego from your true self. The mind and the ego are often intertwined in unproductive ways. By clearing your mind, we begin to see that peace begins with silence. It begins with deep listening, with listening to your own breath instead of the desperate noise of competition, anxiety, and ego. I clear my mind by seeking silence. Let go of how others view you. Find peace and in doing so, find yourself.

1. Let go of either/or

Our minds enjoy separating the world into pairs. There are men and women. Old and young. East and west. Smart and stupid. Rich and poor. Producer and consumer. These pairs are enormously useful for beginners, but they are not helpful if you want to find a lasting and meaningful peace. A peaceful person understands that the world is a most complicated place. They know there is always something to learn, that there are many shades of grey, and many ways to understand behaviour and situation. Accept with humility that there are many universes out there.

Finding peace is as easy as closing your eyes and listening. Listen to the world and you may realize one very profound truth. A peaceful person is one who can listen deeply.

Your heart is beating. There is someone rattling plates in the kitchen. You feel your worries subside. Your heart is beating. It beats slowly. Listen to your heart. Fill it with listening.

Ever meet a peaceful person? They are so beautiful to have around.

Gamification 101

Do you play games? What games do you like to play? Whether you're a golfer, checker whiz, poker player, or Farmville grower, you might be tempted to say that life is game. After all, don't we all just score points and reap the rewards?

The term, gamification, refers to the practice of using the elements of game playing in non-game situations to produce enhanced levels of human engagement. Gamification, in case you didn't know, is impacting many areas of modern life.

Here are four quick examples:

1. On a hybrid vehicle dashboard, a flower begins to grow if you drive in an environmentally conscious fashion.
2. An online newspaper awards writers points on the basis of how many people like and read their work. Points can be translated into money after a threshold has been achieved.
3. Your friend spends real money to buy virtual food and accessories for his virtual pet.
4. You receive a lucrative employment offer based upon the virtual badges you earned by taking free online courses.

To *gamify* something is to add points, badges, leaderboards, and rewards. In other words, fun incentives to human experience. One of the best non-game examples of gamification is the Khan Academy.

The paradigm-breaking Khan Academy provides free online learning videos and has revolutionized education by turning the classroom upside down. The flipped classroom is one where the students watch videos and do computer-marked assignments and then turn to the teacher for personalized assistance.

Khan has added points and badges to many of the courses taken by thousands of elementary and high school students. The result? Adding a fun gaming component has been proven to measurably accelerate learning.

If you've ever used a loyalty card to book a flight, you've already experienced gamification. Come to think of it, I first experienced gamification when I collected Esso power player hockey cards when I was kid.

Gamification is everywhere.

Teachers haven't been the only group to see Khan's tracking data and been amazed. Businesses and non-profits have taken to gamification in ways that go beyond the simplicity of contests and sweepstakes.

Even resort towns like Whistler are creating game-like engagement by providing contests that reward daily participation in a blog in much the same way that we participate in Facebook and social media. In an odd way, this kind of marketing is similar to the flipped classroom because it is consumers who are doing all the work/play, not the marketers. In fact, gamifying organizational innovation is one of the leading applications of this concept.

Need ideas? Make coming up with profitable innovations fun for your employees and customers, and the ideas begin pouring in.

When we do something for fun and we can receive prizes and rewards for doing so, companies are discovering enhanced loyalty.

But more importantly, they are creating product messiahs and evangelists, people who love a product/service so much that they share their glee in unexpected and voluntary and perhaps annoying ways.

In case you're wondering where Facebook may be going, it is probably headed into an advertising/marketing gray area where authentic consumer evangelism reaps a bigger bang for the advertising dollar than simply paying for mouse clicks. In other words, in the future, we will become product advocates through gamification in a way that will allow us to be paid when we get our friends to try or recommend a product or service that we endorse.

The equation is simple. You like a particular brand? Why not get paid for telling your friends about it? Become a top brand advocate, and you get the brand for free. Praise gamification.

As you might have guessed, gamification is about far more than shopping. For example, if you take an online course and do well enough to receive recognition in the form of badge, then participating employers may be convinced the badges are as good or better than a traditional educational credential.

Perhaps one day people will collect online badges as a better way of verifying to an employer they really know their stuff. Of course, it is no wonder the leading universities are striving to get in front of this.

The prospect of a shoulder full of badges may sounds like the Boy Scouts and Girl Guides, but just like those organizations, many are realizing just how much people seem to be motivated and interested in compiling points, receiving rewards, and sewing on (digitally) cool looking badges.

Have you looked at a military uniform lately? Medals, crosses, stars, and badges are used to designate achievement and status.

It doesn't take a rocket scientist to see how engaged people are when they are deep into a game. Think about how effortlessly people learn within a game compared to how difficult it is to put together a barbecue or a set of shelves. Think about the hours spent.

What happens when you make doing challenging things more like a game? Will people be more engaged? Will the velocity of learning rise? Will motivation truly increase?

Will others begin paying you for the privilege of doing their work? Or will it be the other way around? Did you know that our healthcare system and education system are the most popular targets for future gamification? Get points. Increase your score. Get it all free!

One game leads to another game, which is inside a bigger game. And so on.

Sure, life can be pretty fun if you treat it like a game, but how do you know what game you're really playing? Are we really that simple? I will give you free points if you email me.

Dear

Leader

You can't sleep. Greece is falling. Italy is next. California is sinking. Protests everywhere. Connect the dots.

You toss and turn. Your organization needs you. Everyone you talk with says the same thing: uncertainty is the name of the game. What worked before may not work again. Your organization did extremely well from 1997 to 2007, but salaries stayed flat. Costs continue to rise. A storm is brewing.

You get up and look out the window. Globalization has linked everything to everything. Even though you're worrying about your work right now, you suspect that if interest rates go up, your mortgage will kill you. Austerity begins at home, you think. Your children are sleeping. What happens if you start cutting costs?

Businesses are closing. You're trying not to notice, but everybody is holding onto their wallets and purses. Austerity has its downside. The economy shrinks.

Cost-cutting is something you must do, but cost-cutting won't grow the business. Cost-cutting won't leverage your assets.

How do you grow revenues in a time of uncertainty? You're pacing now. Your competitors are probably wondering the same thing. Should you raise prices? Should you seek out new products and new markets? How do you diversify your revenues?

Growth and cost-cutting. The trick is balancing both activities.

Your employees are depending on you. How do you grow for the sake of the whole? Which weaker activities do you stop? It's in the numbers. It's in your gut.

Outside, the street is dark. Frost on windshields. Letting go won't be easy for you. Should you lay people off, put loyal people out of work? What's best for the organization? You've got to mobilize your best people. You need to gather your best team. You need to listen and lead.

There's another problem. You look out the window and see your own reflection. The problem is you. It is your thinking. Your damn habits. You want different results, but you are stuck doing the same old-same old.

You need to behave differently. You need to create a system that rewards and incentivizes new ideas. Okay, you're tired. You're exhausted. Tell yourself the truth, you say. You're too comfortable to make change.

Change one small thing, you say. Start with those small but transformational projects. Start with your thinking.

You consider your friends in government. Everything changes while everything stays the same. Governments come and go. The problems are permanent because the system never changes.

You think about the people in Libya. Your nation applauded the protests. NATO bombed the heck out of the country. You cheer the power of protest, yet you are incredibly intolerant of people protesting in your own city.

Why?

The system has favoured you, but will it favour your children? You've been lucky. Demographics have been on your side. You know retired people that are making well over $100k per year in pensions.

Their houses are paid off. Lucky, deserving, or destructive?

Will Canada be able to compete if we don't do something about the gridlock in government and our own addiction to systems and processes that used to work?

For one clear moment you recognize the truth. The system is working against you. You've got the right people in the wrong jobs. You've got no innovation infrastructure.

Sometimes you can't stand the responsibility. The ship is so hard to steer. You honestly don't know what to do. Should you give up and just go for the quick win? Pad your retirement nest and get the heck out?

No. There are three things you must do. Three major actions.

1. You must grow.
2. You must cut costs.
3. You must improve systems.

You're going sit down with your best thinkers in each area. You're not going to waste a lot of time. You've got to act now. There are opportunities to realize. Yes, it means confronting yourself. It means reaching out. It means courage.

You wonder now about setting up a lunch with a rival to discuss joining forces. Yes, you're going to take your whole team to that conference. Learning is your best response.

You're going to expand the sense of hope.

You say to yourself – a strong body is a strong mind. It's time to focus on your body. It's time to focus on what matters most to you: your health, your family, your organization, your community.

Hey, you're going to vote now. We need good people at all levels of leadership. You're going to ask the candidates about smart growth, cuts, and improvements.

You're starting to feel good. Greece may fail. California may sink. The child poverty rate may rise. You can learn from the protesters. Embrace change.

You can't just spend yourself into prosperity. Greece taught you that. Ontario teaches you that. Your cash-flow problem at home tells you a lot.

You can't grow and innovate through just austerity measures either. Canada teaches you that. Even your accountant tells you that.

You can't achieve lasting prosperity if the system ends up being an obstacle and a drag on innovation. All government teaches you that. The cost of health care teaches you that.

You have a three-part plan. The house is quiet and still. You can hear your heart furiously beating. It's in a balanced approach. Grow. Cut costs. Improve.

This is how you change lives. This is how you create an organization, build a community, and save a country.

The Secret of How to Kill Bureaucracy

Why does managing costs only serve to increase them? Why do performance measures designed to motivate employees almost always fail? Why do most strategic plans get put away only months after the ink has dried? Why do one on ones with people rarely work over the long term? Why do many of us feel so crushed and overwhelmed by the bureaucracy of our organizations?

We spend billions trying to learn how to fix this stuff. Billions spent on consultants and software to track our progress; then we go back to our workplaces and get crushed by the machinery of our own creation.

In service organizations, we scarcely know what to do aside from importing a factory model from Toyota, putting stopwatches in emergency rooms or testing the hell out of our learners.

Canada's national productivity is the envy of no nation. No wonder we're so weary. There is no use trying to empower an individual to go to battle in a system that is crazy. There is only one solution and that is to fix the system.

Systems-thinking for human organizations is perhaps the only way to go. Patients, learners, homeowners, insurers, you name it, who do you really serve? Believe it or not sometimes the honest answer to that question is "I serve the boss's financial metrics."

No wonder wait times are up and learning performance is down. No wonder governments think privatization, amalgamation, and centralization is the answer.

There are so many ways our organizations create waste, but the most boneheaded waste of all is adding additional resources to deal with problems created by a faulty product or service. Whole departments, subsidiaries, and separate companies are created in order to address flaws that originate from the source.

Why not fix the original product or service? If you build a flawed product or service, why do you think spending more money on the response time metrics of your customer service agents in India is going to fix it? If you build a flawed model, it is very tempting to add centralization and targets to your must-do list. Oh yeah, let's buy software that does not add core value.

Offering up targets that have nothing to do with your central purpose is perhaps the second biggest boneheaded waste of all. No wonder it can take seven or more people to badly look after a sick senior or a child in foster care, if each person is only incentivized to check off their list of misaligned targets.

Let the target not be an individual behaviour that you want to speed up; let the target be an organization's central purpose. If you make your target, say, number of customers processed in one hour, then all you will do is create more problems for yourself.

Customers will leave without the complete service. They will return, but they will return angry. You will spend money on the bottlenecks.

Then you will need to create more targets, more departments, and more resources. All because you are basically unable to see the system.

What is the demand for your service? How is it predictable? How can we make sure we train for all the major variations on that demand so that front line people can be successful, and the client can receive increased value?

One size does not fit all. Centralization and standardization only increase costs. And when someone asks a question your frontline can't answer, then bring in an expert to help train the frontline person. Don't create another operation to deal with the failure of your system. Whenever you create a process to deal with service failure, then you will unwittingly drive up costs. That's why managing costs drives up costs.

The greatest mistake of most organizations is failing to understand and communicate purpose.

Every single employee should understand how to create value. When that happens, you don't unwittingly create departments to deal with service failure. Instead, you empower and inspire employees to create the best service possible.

Do you work in a department of failure? It's not fun. You love your team. But no matter how many consultants you bring in or how glowing your performance reviews, a one-on-one pep talk and a pat on the back won't fix the core problem.

Creating a high performance service culture is not about counting up widgets, timing people, publishing strategic plans, or setting measurable targets.

Managing a budget does not create an inspired organization. Managing people alone will not create an inspired organization. It starts and ends with purpose.

If your purpose is to heal people, stop sending seven people who belong to seven different departments, all with competing budgets and metrics.

If your purpose is to educate, stop forcing your learners to make three separate trips to apply and then two more trips to register.

If your purpose is to manage your numbers, drum up the courage to say no, that is not how to lead. Managing costs is a sure way to inflate costs and drive morale down.

7 Ways to Strengthen Your Organization

1. Clarify your central purpose so that every employee understands their connection to it.
2. Measure the demand for your value proposition (product, service, program)
3. Understand your demand so that you can predict how to maximize successful transactions.
4. Set your employees free to meet the demand.
5. Continuously improve your service using a systems approach.
6. Fix the source and avoid adding resources to fix the products of failure.
7. Use purpose to create a system that continuously adds value and eliminates waste.

The Glory of the Second Time

The first kiss. The first house. The first child. The first, the first, oh the first. How we live for a world of first times.

The anxiety builds. Your heart quickens. You wonder if you will succeed or fail. The first time you do anything, you cannot help but feel the extra excitement. But the extra anxiety lurks behind that first corner.

Although first times are so often celebrated by our culture, let us give praise to the underrated second time. Let us say, the second time, not the first time, can be the best time.

Poor old second time; often ignored and never celebrated. The second child often lurks in the shadow of the first. The second love is forced to live up to the turbulence of the first. The second experience often never making it to the level of the first.

Poor old second time.

But the second kiss is often better than the first. The second time to that vacation spot, after you've worked out all the kinks, is often less eventful, but much more relaxed.

Now you know the shortest walk to the beach. Now you know where best to kiss. Nuzzle that second time. Ah, beautiful second time. How can you beat where you have already scouted the best parking?

Why not respect the second time?

Some say the world can be divided between the adventurers and the homebodies. The adventurers want to till new ground. They seek new places and new experiences. They enjoy the excitement of the first time.

They say, "Hey, let's hear it for the first time. Life is a new golf course every morning. The world is big enough so that repeating an experience is merely a chance wasted."

On the other hand, the homebodies prefer routine. They enjoy rhythm and overlooked conveniences like bowel regularity and the pleasure of knowing exactly where you are. They enjoy knowing the name of their neighbourhood baker, sushi chef, and barista.

They say the second time builds community. The joy of the first time is over-rated. Ritual deepens our experiences and enhances our relationships.

In the course of your daily life, how many first times do you actually get? Many of us live our lives in deep grooves. We say with a deep sigh, there are few, if any, first or second times.

But perhaps the modern life of ritual and routine contains within it many opportunities to experience the new. Isn't every breath new? Isn't it possible to kiss or be kissed in a spot that is new, whether we're talking about that freckled spot on the shoulder or that picnic bench on that sandy shore?

Isn't it possible to discover a place in your own community where you have never enjoyed coffee? Isn't it possible to drink what you've never drunk before, eat what you have never ordered, and step where you have never stepped?

Do you even have time to leave the beaten path in your comfortable Velcro shoes and seek something new for that eternally special first time? First times are scary and quite exhausting.

Then there are all those places to visit for the second time. The places you are now perhaps ready for, those experiences, like that challenging literary novel or that abstract piece of art or that attempt to write a poem. Isn't it possible that you're ready for that long avoided reunion?

A second time, after a bad experience, can read you. The experience can be a measure of your level of maturity. Who knows what that second time will bring you? Perhaps you can write. Perhaps you possess more talent that you thought. Perhaps your body is more capable. Your heart more open.

The second time is like the first chance. The second time may be your first shot at seeing yourself anew. Why don't we respect the second time? Is it because it often follows the sting of failure?

You stay away from the second time, especially if the first time was a fumbled mess. There is no second kiss if the first one banged teeth and sent lightning to your spine. There is no second attempt at poetry if your teacher cringed or snorted behind her back.

But there are those brave few who refuse to accept a spoiled first time. I know many who have discovered themselves through a stubborn attachment to the second time. They found their first times were miscalculations. A bad first time can give you the wrong idea about yourself.

The second kiss. The second batch. The second child. The second math course. The second attempt. The second book. The second try. The second career. The second hug.

Embrace the glory of the second time. Friends from high school become lovers thirty years later. A 50-year old artist discovers that her fear of math was totally unfounded.

Second times can tell you a lot about yourself. The second time can speak to you in a glorious and surprisingly beautiful way. There is much more to you than you might imagine.

It was the best of times. It was the worst of times. It will be the second best of times that make you.

The second time may be the best time of all. Say it again.

The Difference Between Me and You

The most courageous act of all is to be honest with yourself: my happiness is dependent on your misery.

We have a name for the difference between you and the person below you. Let's call it privilege. One thing about privilege is that it is easily offended.

I find it amazing how hurt we are by that person below us. It is often the perpetrator of the pain who ends up seeking compensation from the victim. Why is the victim always asked to apologize?

"I'm sorry," says the victim. "Sorry the pain you caused me makes you feel so bad."

I know something about my sense of privilege. It comes with an endless sense of entitlement. Powerful people are ignorant of the damage they do. They are always the victim. They want gratitude, even from the people they have harmed.

"It's the system," they say.

"Profit is when I put in less and take out more," they say. "Damnit, don't you see I make the world turn!"

I am bitter about these people because I may be one of them.

We who are privileged retain a self-righteous sense of

ambivalence. This is the pyramid of privilege, we say. And with this thinking comes the insistence that poverty is deserved.

No, poverty is a necessary condition of our system.

How can it be wrong to set the hurt person from the hurt culture on a path toward self-reliance? Why does it hurt the privileged to see such gifts given freely?

Why does it hurt the privileged to have tax subsidies reduced while at the same time raging against social support and health care which are subsidies, too?

Why does it hurt to be kind to your fellow travellers?

How is it possible that we feel sorry for the bullies? Please, bank, take this interest free loan of billions. Please, senator, we forgive your disregard for public funds. After all, you are one of the privileged.

Why are we so hard done by when someone dares ask us to contribute something more?

I have felt this unbelievable urge to be offended when my privilege is challenged. I don't want my illusions questioned. The truth is that I am nothing. I am nothing.

My world of possessions. My badges of honour. Authority. What happens when I stop comparing? What happens when we stop trying to create more losers and realize that competition is meaningless?

There is no You. There is only We.

That honed body. That comfort. That luxurious life. What will climbing Mount Accumulation feel like when you are done? Your boat is a bit longer. Your office a bit bigger. Your face more tanned.

You are nothing without that Other person. The one in the gutter. You don't really exist until your foot is on his neck. You need your victim.

How do we live without subjugation? Happiness is surely more. Who are we without our privileges and victims? In truth, you are really no different than your victim.

Any decent sociologist can look at your parents and birthday and predict the type of cheese in your refrigerator, the vintages of your wine collection, the shining brand of your soul.

You have been programmed to believe your happiness is determined by the distance between you and that Other: that immigrant worker, that indigenous protestor, that mythical family who wants your life.

Imagine a world burned by our own recklessness, a surface made bereft by fracking and foolishness. Our planet is demarcated by rich and poor, north and south, east and west, urban and rural. It is defined by how much better I am than you.

If the world burned would happiness still rest on the height of your stash? If the world ended, would you still measure yourself by another's misery? What would matter? Would you still be you?

I want to stop taking advantage of you. I want to stop distancing myself from you.

The system is broken. Profit does not cause happiness. Let us count down the Last Days of Privilege.

The distance between you and that disabled human, between you and that cursed foreigner, between you and the Other . . . it does not exist.

The Most Deadly Silence of All

Do you have a workplace enemy? You walk into the meeting room, and you can feel it in your bones. You are not wanted.

Your attempts at conversation seem forced. Every time you speak, the person turns away. The eyes roll. The disdains spills. Worse still, the work is starting to suffer.

And it's starting to get personal with you, too. You're tired of being ignored or worse, and you feel that your input is no longer valued. Your health may even be impacted. How do you deal with workplace silence?

Silence is the enemy of the work. Work is a social place. It's a place that thrives on sound. The sound of laughter. The sound of debate. The fury of engagement. The inspiration of trusting dialogue.

When all that is left is silence, not only are you in deep trouble, but so might your career. Silence may be a temporary truce, until the emotions settle and wisdom prevails. But it can also be a sign of giving up, of stasis, of frozen hearts. When all that is left is silence, we must listen very carefully.

It takes emotional courage to acknowledge your heart is frozen at the workplace. It is far easier and more likely you will go to your boss or fellow colleagues and begin the blame game.

It is always more difficult to acknowledge your own role in the silence. It is more difficult to search your own history. Most people have emotional triggers that are often unconsciously released by certain kinds of conflict.

For example, I don't like bullies. When I was a child, I was bullied and teased a lot because I was a Korean Canadian. When I see a workplace bully now, it is very difficult for me not to become the aggressor, a veritable bully myself.

There are stories about my sense of kindness and fairness; we all have similar stories. But there are also stories about how I deal with certain kinds of conflicts, stories that do not fill me with pride.

The victim should not respond by bullying. The bully can also be bullied. The dance between victim and aggressor is a deeply ambivalent and complex one.

At the workplace, I recommend three approaches in dealing with silence.

The first step is to simply acknowledge when you detect discomfort around a colleague. The acknowledgement puts you in a position to think about what is triggering your sensitivities. By naming your distress, by taking on the position of learner not judger, you are potentially able to see it, reflect upon it, and examine it.

The second step is extremely difficult. Do you have the ability to share in a non-threatening way how you experience the other person? This skill requires a kind of philosophical acknowledgement or ability, the ability to acknowledge another person's reality as different from your own.

The third skill is to find shared understanding with yourself (and preferably with the other person if they are willing) about the key differences in your self-perception and in the other's perception of you. Understanding these differences help us to hear and grow in our appreciation of each other.

What does understanding look like? It is not a blind acceptance of the other's point of view as much as it is an acceptance that a complete view of reality is not possible, that sharing our perspectives is the best way to serve the workplace and the best way to achieve mutual goals.

Sharing through dialogue, our different perceptions, in a manner that is respectful and safe, is also the best way to be together in any enterprise.

The three skills combined remain the hallmark of highly skilled managers, professionals, parents, teachers, and coaches. They begin with knowing oneself in terms of your own history and culture. They end in respectful dialogue that potentially ends the silence and builds the relationship for more encounters, more engagement, and stronger understanding of differences.

In the end what remains is simply this: an authentic partnership between two people.

Without this partnership, no relationship and no organization can function to a high level, let alone blossom into something inspiring.

Partnership means, more than anything else, a commitment to acknowledging the truth of your own experience, practicing courageous dialogue in the moment, and finally, accepting the truth and wisdom of holding multiple perspectives.

Professionally, personally, in any area of human endeavor

partnership, it moves at only one speed: the speed of authentic commitment to dialogue.

Sometimes silence can exist even when there appears to be a great deal of talking. Silence can be the absence of authentic feeling in any communication.

Let the silence be heard.

For you, for your organization, for your team, for your marriage, for our planet – let the silence be heard.

Three Things Indigenous People Taught Me

> "If you have come here to help me, you are
> wasting your time. But if you have come because
> your liberation is bound up with mine,
> then let us walk together."
> *Australian Aboriginal Activists Group 1970s*

This is my personal prayer. It may offend immigrants who think assimilation is fine. It may offend settler Canadians who believe they have done no wrong. If this offends you, I am sorry.

There are three things I learned from my Indigenous sisters and brothers.

Now I have learned a lot of things in my life. But these three things exist on a higher plane than the degrees beside my name, my years as a teacher, and my time as a so-called educational leader.

Before I studied and reflected upon the indigenous ways of knowing, I was but a child. Before I go further I acknowledge that Indigenous knowledge is not necessarily race or culture based. Being a member of a culture doesn't guarantee you wisdom unless you've walked the long journey.

Many Indigenous people are still learning what it means to live according to an Indigenous worldview. And many non-aboriginal people are hostile to questioning the roots of their own thinking and being.

It is all about the journey.

My journey into the cultural and social history of my Korean upbringing brings me to a deeper understanding of my parents and ancestors. I didn't care so much about my history when I was young. I was torn. I wanted desperately to be normal, just like you.

When you reflect upon the person you have become you begin to hear the voices of your ancestors. Mine tell me one very clear thing: the human family is one.

This knowledge is the core of what can be called the Indigenous worldview. (A deeper view contends that we are also one with all of life.) It isn't difficult to understand why Indigenous people all over the globe are fiercely protective of the land. It is a core part of their identity. I pray to make it a part of mine.

After I reflected upon my own connection to the land, I realized that my culture taught me that the land was simply for my personal use. No wonder there are fewer species, fewer natural places.

The second thing I have learned from my Indigenous sisters and brothers is to respect the connection between mind, spirit, and body. I had learned in my culture to gorge on book wisdom, ignore my body's appetite for knowledge, and be suspicious of the spirit.

I realize now that it is folly to separate your mind from your body, that the body contains great wisdom that connecting the mind, body, and the spirit can heal what is broken.

I have enjoyed more than 50 years of life. My children teach me.

I have read many books. I held both parents before they died. But something inside me (and perhaps outside of me) feels so broken.

If you need a healing journey where do you start? When you reflect upon the past, your future changes.

The third piece of wisdom I learned was to question my own worldview, the symbolic air that I breathe, the cultural identity that fixes me, the corporate society that teaches us we are what we consume and there is but one way to live.

Are there other ways?

Yes, this journey is a reinvention; it requires imagination, and yes, you won't know the answers before the journey begins. Each journey is unique.

Understanding the worldview that got us here might be the great hope of this world. It will make us aware of how to resist the powerful forces that tell us the master/servant relationship is the only way to live, that tells us women are lesser than men, that tells us that nature is for our own use, that tells us the economy is not for us, that tells us to give up the journey before we start.

Most people travel (even between cultures) under one dominant worldview that contains one's values, beliefs, and ideology. Indigenous people face the rupture caused when one worldview tries to extinguish another. Cultural assimilation is one thing; extinguishing a worldview may be quite another.

But it survives after 500 years on feathers, circles, fish soup, Twitter feeds, treaties, and land leases.

An Indigenous worldview teaches us one overwhelming idea: We can change the way we think, so that we can live in harmony with ourselves and this planet. Otherwise, we can only hope for more of the same.

More suicides. More shootings. More wars. More spills. More languages lost. More sadness. More men in jail. More children and women living alone.

Idle No More may seem like a fad. It may appear to have no goals or no agenda. You will definitely see one chief say it is good and one say it is bad.

One day we will realize that this journey is relational, that life is about our relationships, with our families, with our culture, with our civilization.

My journey tells me that adopting a deeper awareness and consciousness of who we are, how we can heal, and how we can hope for a better world is why Idle No More is not just about the freedom and rights of Indigenous people in Canada. It is about freedom for us all.

I am an ally of a deeper and more profound relationship with ourselves and with our planet. I was a child before I learned the change begins with you. Who are you? What kind of world do you want? Where is the hope?

Let us find a way to transcend the way we think about the human family.

This is a prayer for my Indigenous sisters and brothers. I am a Korean Canadian, the son of Ji Won and Sook Chung. We acknowledge the traditional territories of First Nation, Metis, and Inuit people. We respect all Indigenous Peoples.

We will be idle no more.

Talk to Me:

For Parents

and Children

Your father called last night. He told me what a beautiful baby you were. He remembered holding you in his arms. He remembered feeding you, rubbing his face on your belly, and playing with your fingers and toes.

Your mother called last night. She told me how it felt like eternity for you to be born. She remembers bathing you and watching you smile especially when you saw her each morning. She will never stop thinking about you.

I remembered you last night, my child. I remembered everything about you. How much I miss you. How much I love you. How I cannot bear to be apart from you.

You love. And love you again. How many times a day does this happen, when you think about each other without knowing it? And when you do see each other, you don't know what to say, often asking after each other politely as if you were strangers.

Your father called last night. He has never stopped loving you. Your mother told me how much she smiles when she thinks of you.

And you? You know, how much it all means to you, how easily things can change, not just from good to bad but from bad to good.

Your parents love you. And yet. And yet…

Your mother talked to me last night. She knows you find her irritating. Shall we tell her why?

Your father talked to me last night. He knows he makes you lose your patience. Shall we tell him why?

Shall we fill the air with judgment? Shall we fill the air with why your parents cannot be this or that? Or shall we talk about the cold day when you won't be able to say a single word to them?

When they are no more.

Many don't learn to love their parents until it is too late. Our impatience with them begins inside of us. We are impatient with ourselves, with where we are, with our expectations of ourselves.

My parents expect too much, you say, that's why you can't stand them.

Your mother and father called last night. They would like to hear from you. All they want to do is love you.

Why can't you let them?

Do you feel the resistance inside you? Child, you are still growing up. You are still learning to realize who you really are and where you came from.

Child, call your parents tonight, and tell them what it feels like to experience their love.

Father, your love is beautiful, but it makes me feel like a failure. I feel like I can never please you. That makes me feel like such a disappointment in your eyes.

Mother, your love is beautiful, but it makes me feel smothered. I feel like you will never let me grow up. That makes me feel like a child in your eyes.

I see. I hear you. I love you child. We can both be better.

But know one thing: parents have a funny way of growing up when you grow up. And children have a funny way of growing up when you grow up.

To be grown up is to stop judging and begin accepting difference. You see the world differently. I see that, I accept that, I love that.

The paradox of life is the pain of love. You do not grow up without learning how give and receive love. Giving and receiving. You cannot give love while sitting alone. You cannot receive love while thinking about it.

Love is a performance. It happens as a dialogue between two people who are committed not to the truth, or honesty, or family, or any single concept or idea, other than the commitment to be in dialogue.

Talk to me.

My father called last night. It was only a dream, but I cried and cried.

Oh, Father, how much I love you. Oh, Mother. Oh, how I wish you could see me now, so I could hold you in my arms and tell you what a sweet mother you have always been to me.

How to Make the World a Better Place

Change! Everybody is talking about change. Managing change. Innovating change. Leading change. Work change. Lifestyle change. Spiritual change. As they say, the only thing constant in the world is change.

A stroll in your public library tells us this topic is of great interest. Whether we want to lose 25 lbs or orchestrate an initiative that will change a city, shape a nation, or inspire the world; there appears to be an endless appetite for transformation. Here are five principles for engaging in a change initiative.

Principle 1: Connect every change goal to an inspiring purpose

Why did you choose your particular change agenda? Why do you want to change? Of all the things you could do why does this initiative mean the most? Goals are sometimes connected to a strong purpose, and sometimes they are not. Sometimes we attempt to create a goal for something that is disconnected from us. You may lack energy around the goal and wonder why. It may be someone else's purpose. It may not utilize your talents.

Most tantalizingly troublesome of all is the change goal that seems great, feels connected to purpose, but ultimately fails to inspire. Inspiration is the secret. If you can combine your change goal with an inspiring purpose, then you will accomplish a lot more than trying to start a flame, you will stoke a roaring fire.

Principle 2: Accept change advice from those who've been there

Stephen Covey talks about change from the inside out. Mahatma Gandhi exhorted us to be the change we want to see in the world. The principle of walk the talk, authentic change, and soul-based change begins with the notion that the best change agent to learn from is one that has already been on the journey. That's why General Managers like to hire NHL coaches that have once been professional players. We like people who have been there and done that.

On the other hand, that's why people don't particularly enjoy being led by those who haven't been there. Would a surgeon take surgical advice from someone who has never been there? But it's amazing how many artists take advice from people who have never sold a painting or bought an original. It's amazing how many who face retirement take advice from people who have never been there.

Be careful who you take change advice from. Well-meaning amateurs have limited value as coaches on your change journey.

Principle 3: Reflect upon the blessings of the journey

No change goal worth achieving will be without its bumps and detours. The best way to manage one's inspiration is to reflect regularly. Why does this goal mean so much to me? What can I celebrate as a milestone achieved? How am I managing by inspiration? What am I learning along with the way about myself, about how I achieve my goals, about how I lead my own self transformation?

A common yet highly effective tool is the journal. Counsellors use them for their clients, and they use journals themselves to help surface and guide their thoughts and feelings.

Possibly the most powerful journal practice of them all is the gratitude journal. Just spend ten minutes writing down what you are grateful for. Such a small seemingly inconsequential act has been demonstrated to be life-saving with the potential to impact one's engagement and sense of well-being. The journal is your secret to change success.

Principle 4: Change the story

Our arc and shape of our lives are partially determined by the cultural and social forces of society. How we are raised, what we believe, the values and behaviours that guide our sense of what is acceptable; these things are not created by individuals. On the contrary, they are normalized by groups. This socialized reality is formed as well as challenged by the stories we tell. Our stories tell us who we are, and they tell us who we are not.

Often the story we tell about ourselves can unintentionally limit us. Minorities of one kind or another have been told, "You can't do that. That's not for you." But change marches on. It is only in this century that children were not slaves, women were not second class citizens, and that visible and invisible minorities were given the protection of the law.

Change is possible when we change the story we tell and the story that others tell about us. For change to succeed, we ourselves must change any stories that limit us or prevent us from believing we can succeed.

Why do so many people think they can't paint or do math

or be creative? These self-limiting stories are often the first step toward change. Yes, you can! The secrets to change are locked in the ideologies and assumptions buried in the stories we tell.

Principle 5: Invest in the Moment

Are you one of the people who exchanges your life for money? In one way or another, we all do. Is your life worth the time you devote to making money? Or do you think that you are not receiving enough value for the time you give up? Are you satisfied with how you spend your time? Are you spending your life on the things that matter?

Changing your sense of time may be the most important change you ever make.

Are you one of those people that worries a lot about what happened? Do you spend time worrying about the future? When you focus on the past or the future, one thing is clear: you are allowing the present moment to slip through your fingers.

The present moment is the true wealth of your existence.

Invest in the moment by doing one very simple but exceedingly difficult practice: live in the now. Attend to the now and all your change moments can succeed. In a single moment, you can make the best choices. In a single moment, you can engage in truly listening and loving another person.

In a single moment, you can transform yourself into the person that you want to be.

No change initiative can succeed if you cannot live it in the moment. By practicing living in the moment, I truly believe all things, all change initiatives, are possible.

Good luck with your self-change. Whether you want a healthier lifestyle, more creative work, improved relationships, or simply find yourself a kinder person, these five secrets to change leadership can help you realize your goals.

Tincture:

The History of Now

Like a bottle around a neck, like a raindrop upon a petal, I keep you in a little bit of liquid. In the little bit of you is a little bit of your mother. High cheek boned and proud. And a little bit of your father. On a ship to Canada from Holland where he will meet and romance your grieving mother.

And in that tincture there is also a little bit of me, too, since we've been together for many years. And, yes, somewhere in that concentrate are my ancestors and yours. Toiling. Hoping. Travelling. All those tomorrows yet to come.

There is my frail grandfather, the son of a feudal lord in another century, who led a peasant village on Jeju Island between Korea and Japan.

And my grandmother, the born again Christian who couldn't read, who made us dandelion salad in Williams Lake and taught me about the pearl divers and fighting kites. The villagers forced them together in 1930, a peasant girl and a lord who died a few years later.

Your aunt, too, is in this concentration, the tall one who was captured by the Japanese in Indonesia, the one who made us nasi goreng in Prince George, the one whose cheekbones I love. A Dutch woman guarded by Korean POWs in a Japanese prison camp.

In every piece of you, there is a little piece of me. And in this tincture, there are generations and generations of our families, joined by war, joined by our wedding on a log platform in Prince George and our children laughing behind the Pazdernik's boat in Kelowna . . . all touched by memory and history.

The more diluted the mixture becomes the more I realize that there is a little bit of everyone in all of us. Yes, you, dear reader. You too, are in everything; in every single drop that ever existed.

Do you remember the taste of abalone and sky on Jeju Island freshly opened by your great grandmother? What taste is on your lips as you summon the past? Or is it the future just out of reach?

And what is that on your lips? The heat of Sambal, the hot mixture of Indonesian spices, carried by your ancestors from Holland to Indonesia, your uncles and great uncles part of the journey across the oceans. The great wars. The great journeys. The great . . . is your love great?

In every single drop of morning dew, every family is revealed as one, every family belongs to every family, each to each. Each breath containing each breath.

Our voices meet across time and enters the laughter of our children, who meet, find their own love, grow old, and add to our tincture. How beautiful and painful it is to grow old, to witness the seasons and see ourselves fade.

Let us not forget the wounds of our families. The tortured battles. The brutality of short, tough lives. The sadness we can feel on a perfect summer day.

Do you sometimes feel the pride, too? The joy in your bones that belongs, strangely, to another time and place and person? The squatted rice picking and the proud storekeeping. And the war ships and sailing boats and sudden picnics. Mustard and princesses.

Really. Who are you really?

What do you see between dreaming and waking? What do you taste when you dive deep into the waters?

This healing tincture, the splashing of wrens, is the ocean of human love, our ancestral joining, a little boy and girl being born to us in the Prince George hospital, a pink cast, a thousand tennis balls, the plastic tablecloth that becomes an umbrella, an old bicycle seat stuffed with a wool sock, the ocean at Willows Beach where you caught crab on your paddle board, the rusty generations of trusty things – cars, bikes, tents, pots, pans, stoves – that held us together and helped us count the years. And released us under the colours of history.

This tincture, the faint drop on the wind that strikes your forehead and you look up. And wonder. Yes, this is our lives. This is now. This is all there is. And, yes, it is fine.

The rain on the windshield is all time past, present, and future. The many universes of our desire, our coolness and warmness, our fingers entwined, our bodies encircled, our lives moving through space.

We are the human family. In a tear or a raindrop or a snowflake or a spot of tea with a biscuit. This is all there is.

I missed you before we met. Even before we met, I think we already were. There is no letting go for us. Because we have always, always been. And will always be.

I miss you.

Hold on. Look straight into your loved ones' eyes and hold on. Do not be afraid of love. Find intimacy. Tears reward the brave. This history is now. Like a bottle around a neck, like a raindrop upon a petal, I keep you in a little bit of liquid.

The

Bubble Man

"When I let go of what I am,
I become what I might be"
Lao Tsu

It is Sunday morning. We've just finished our coffee at the Cornerstone Cafe. An orange cat sits in a window above the street. The cat watches a bubble float by. It floats as large as a children's party balloon. I watch the fragile bubble soar above the street and then disappear.

Another bubble passes over us. It flashes and wobbles in the September wind. The morning light shines across its delicate metallic surface.

Last night I dreamed I was someone else.

For a few moments, we don't know where these huge bubbles are coming from, but soon we see him standing on the corner. There he is. A man with a white beard, suspenders, jeans, and a yellow wand. He dips the wand into his yellow scabbard.

Terry Wilson, 65, is the bubble man.

An elderly couple walks by and then points to the series of bubbles in the sky. A family pushing a stroller stops. The orange cat in the window watches.

A few more people gather. People start chatting. We are smiling. Bubbles, you can't resist them. Their shape-shifting delicacy. Their immediacy. And the fact they disappear with a sparkle and a poof.

Who is the maker of these delights? Who is this transformer of community, this Sunday morning prophet of spontaneity? Is he an artist? Is he a performer who uses bubbles to tell us of the wonder that is *now*?

Or is he simply a lonely man who has found a way to give in a way that seems harmless, inconsequential, but is really an act of the heart?

When we look in wonder at the bubbles floating across the sky, I wonder about what I am doing with my life. The bubble man knows what he is doing. Is my own work as meaningful? Is my work inspiring to others? Am I inspired?

And what if I am not?

All I know is that sometimes I feel as if I am in some unnamed and pointless battle. All my money and effort go into a life that appears to have its own trajectory. The oppressive bills, the steep quest for advancement, my inability to become a more loving person. Yes, I know what it is that I share with the man with bow and quiver.

I am in a bubble, too.

The bubble of the ego. The bubble that dictates what you think and feel. The bubble that says you are right, and others are wrong. The bubble of certainty. The bubble that separates us.

How to be more loving?

The bubble makes you think there will be time enough to choose your life, to be who you want, before it all disappears. With a sparkle and a poof.

186

There can be no change, either personally or socially, if we can't escape our own bubbles. Our current thinking created the world we live in. Our current thinking got us here in this bubble of ecological disaster and selfish materialism.

The world cannot change unless we break the bubble of our own perceptions and assumptions.

How do we change what is inside us?

How do we burst the bubble of ego?

How do we let ourselves go?

How do we stop ourselves from thinking that says: me first. My greed first. My need to be right first. My family first. My party first. My country first. And what, I say, is wrong with all of this?

Einstein said we cannot solve problems with the same mindset that created them. Doing the same thing repeatedly will not produce different results. We face overwhelming challenges as a species.

Do we think we can change?

On Sunday, we saw the bubble man, went for a hike, visited an art gallery, and watched television. The bubbles work like art. For me, the bubbles, those delicate, shape-shifting forms, represent a new way of imagining.

The bubbles are like inspiration itself. In the moment, you delight in them, but then you forget. You live in the next moment, and you forget what you have learned. Inspiration seems so fleeting, so slippery. It's like going to church and falling asleep with your eyes open.

The words flowing over you seem inspiring enough, but you can't get that feeling back again.

Yesterday I dreamed I was someone else. He was just like me, except he was more inspired. He was just like me, except he remembered the lesson of impermanence, mutability, and fragility.

He refused to live inside the bubble.

It is another late night. I cannot sleep. My wife's hand is warm inside mine. I get up and walk around the house. The clock flashes 2 a.m.

The light of the moon reflects against the kitchen wall. My problem is not with the world but with me. How can I be different? How can I be a better leader, a better father, a better husband, a better member of the community?

What will be my sword and scabbard? How do I transform myself?

The wind moves through the poplar trees outside the window. I want to lose you, I say to myself. A better life does not mean the same life. I am writing this because I want to lose Stan Chung. The bubble floats and disappears. I need to let go of who I am to be the person I want to be. I am losing you.

Let go.

Letter to

My Children

You are both still pretty young, but should that stop me from giving you unsolicited advice? Hey, what are fathers for? I want to offer this advice because I am just old enough to give fairly decent advice and just young enough to remember it.

First of all, my son and daughter, success has nothing to do with intelligence. Sure, there are lots of not too bright people out there robbing stores and leaving their wallets behind, but for the most part, success isn't about innate talent.

IQ is a bad predictor of who will find happiness on the road of life. Plenty of smart people will not translate their brains into grades. And even more people will not translate their grades into a great career.

Ask kindergarten teachers. They can tell you with good accuracy which kid is going to med school, which kid is going to struggle, and which kid is headed to prison. This, of course, begs the question: if we can peg a kid that young, why can't we do something about it?

No matter how much early childhood education we give a child, there is still the question of a child's trajectory. That kid is only going to go so far. It's sad actually, because we would really like to think we can change a person's trajectory.

So what is this predictor of success that teachers use? What is this secret that can indicate whether a child is headed toward a life of reward or a life of imprisonment?

Life success, if you really want to know, has something to do with what researchers call self-regulation. What is self-regulation? Here's my take on it.

1. Do you know how to wait? Can you delay gratification in order to wait for something really good instead of settling for an immediate reward? In other words, do you have patience? If you are five or 50 and you can't wait for things, like Christmas morning and trips to the drugstore for condoms, chances are life will be pretty difficult.

2. Do you know how to sleep? Now that seems so simple, but many five and 50 year olds have difficulty with sleep. If you think about it, going to bed requires complex self-regulation. You have to be able to physically monitor your energy. You have to say no to the rest of the day. You have to understand the consequences of not going to bed. If you don't teach a child to sleep, there are life-long consequences.

3. Do you know how to eat? Again, some five-years-olds effortlessly know how to feed themselves with nutritious food. Some 50 year olds have a very complex relationship with food, a relationship that influences their ability to regulate their senses, their emotions, and their minds. Ask anyone, eating right is not easy.

4. Do you know how to think? A five-year-old who has been raised well can out-think a negative emotion. The resilient youngster can deal with rejection or failure by understanding that failure is not permanent, that hard

work, more learning, and better collaboration can lead to success next time. There are many 50 year olds who can't think through their negative emotions. They think failure is permanent. They think life is against them. They think they can't change.

5. Do you know how to find calmness? Without calmness it is difficult to learn and to live. Without calmness it is nearly impossible to feel, to think, to love, and to be mindful. Calmness is not a biochemical problem to be cured by drugs or video games; instead, it requires practice, study, and reflection.

These five types of regulation only skim the surface of this emerging area of research. However, the most important thing to know about self-regulation is that it is changeable. It can be improved.

There is always hope.

There is nothing more important than the quality of love you receive as a child and no knowledge more important than your ability to regulate yourself.

Love is not just a nice option; in fact, love is a necessity for the successful formation of an ever-evolving brain that is ever-capable of learning, adapting, and growing.

A brain that learns is a brain that is loved. Neuroscientists are making it pretty clear that love makes our brains grow. Love makes us better able to sense the world. Love connects our body to our senses and to our ability to reason.

What is love? First of all, loving is touching. It is listening. It is smiling. It is being there. It is modeling self-regulation.

Love is patient. Love is kind. It is never too late to love.

I am very proud of you. You do well in school. We taught you how to wait, how to sleep, how to eat, and how to think about your emotions. I hope you do the same thing with your children.

But what I'd like to confess is that your father is still learning to do all the things I have tried to teach you.

At my age, I must still practice self-regulation. I must still remember that hard work is more important than luck. That patience will be rewarded. And that love is everything.

A New of Way of Living: Social Innovation?

Look across the ocean at the missiles of pain. At exploding limbs. Hear the cries of children in our own communities. Watch the hand-wringing and pontification of our leaders. The complaints of transnational gridlock.

Recognize the generational struggle of our home grown refugees: First Nations, Metis and Inuit. The finger pointing. Excuses galore. So much division. So much to unlearn.

I know I must help, not just others, but myself. Change one – change many. And yes, change myself, too.

The bottom line is how do I unlearn so many things?

Unlearn patriarchy, racism, colonialism and unkindness. Unlearn my core addictions: pacifying myself with the sugar of success. Oh, the great temptation of comfort. Oh, the unshakeable assumption of our separateness.

Confession 1: Sometimes, I think it is too late for me.

Confession 2: I have not yet shown my children an economic model for a new way of living.

Let's take a moment to understand how many entrepreneurs are becoming *social entrepreneurs*. What are social entrepreneurs?

Social entrepreneurs address our social issues through innovation. They are hybrids who use their entrepreneurial talents for public good. They are driven to make an impact upon people and planet.

Who are they? Ask the United Way. Ask craftspeople, social workers and typeface designers. Go to church basements and speak to community leaders. Often, they start as volunteers assisting communities in finding better ways to come together.

In Victoria, social entrepreneurs created community theatre on bicycles (Theatre SKAM). In north Winnipeg, social entrepreneurs opened their gardens for neighbours to sell produce on Main Street (Neechi Commons). In Edmonton, they created a fund to catalyze entrepreneurial ideas on social change. In Toronto, there are hundreds of social start-ups and incubators for nearly every sector (socialinnovation.org).

You might be a social entrepreneur without knowing it. Maybe you've had your neighbours over to organize something. You blog and read local blogs. You recycle when you want to recycle. You share for the sake of sharing.

People think you're crazy. Not that crazy, because leading corporations want aboard, too. We should all want under the social innovation tent. For the sake of the child. For the sake of the human family. For us.

Social entrepreneurs invent new solutions for humanity. The world's first 3D printer for prosthetic limbs prints off a new arm for Daniel, a Sudanese boy with no arms (notimpossiblelabs.com).

By doing this work, these people disrupt the way things are currently done. Social entrepreneurs, in the effort to help one person, often end up figuring out a way to serve many. They may uncover a new channel for distributing services, novel processes to engage community and, as a result, innovate designs for a better way of life.

Colleges are teaching it. Governments are funding it. Social innovation is on the rise. If there is one cardinal principal of social innovation it is this: help one, help many.

How easy it is to help one person?

I warn myself daily of the pitfalls of trying to help. Helping someone else can be toxic to the other person. You can harm by helping, not realizing that you are enabling dependence.

Helping someone can take your ego to new heights. You ask what's in it for you. We all have seen selflessness shift into entitlement. Unlearning this is the practice of a lifetime.

Confession 3: The best way to help is to walk beside someone as an equal, as a fellow traveller on the journey of life.

We hunger for change, but we forget how impossible it is to change even the smallest of our habits. How can you change the world, if you're still so addicted to the current business model of your life? How can you shift consciousness, if you're still hanging onto unworkable ideas and behaviours?

Does your life business model keep people apart, find motivation in selfishness, and serve to indulge your pursuit of fear/comfort/competition?

Today, communities are innovating the old business model that sacrifices people for profits. Germany generates 20 per cent of its energy through solar power. Canada generates one per cent. We look to social entrepreneurs to innovate for humanity.

Take a breath. The older I get, the easier it is to fool myself. Do I dare sacrifice my need for comfort? I like my possessions. I like my stuff.

But the world is so rich. Most of us have much more than we need. How can I ask others to let go unless I do? Is there refuge in letting go of things we don't really need? Is there solace in deeper sharing? I don't know.

I have let go of house, career and certain fixed ideas of success. I can tell you I have never been more frightened.

Nor have I ever felt freer.

I have never felt more alive to possibility.

Today, I begin the journey toward conscious and active social innovation. I will start by becoming an entrepreneur of my own soul.

Are you ready? Join us, today, in committing our talents and knowledge toward innovation for humanity.

Start with you. Be mindful of who you are and where you came from. Start with this question: What kind of world do you want to live in?

The Courage to be Altered by Strangers

In Canada, when we think of international students, we usually recall they pay a much higher tuition. This allows high schools and post-secondary institutions some financial relief.

In the United States, international students are thought of in similar terms, but they focus on talent acquisition. The plan is to bring their talents to the American innovation ecosystem.

China used to send their students all over the globe. But in a few years, China will have reached an equilibrium, and in five years or so, more students will be going to China than coming abroad.

Why are international students flocking to China?

If you live in one of the Southeast Asian or African countries, you're worried about all this brain drain. But even that seemingly tough problem is changing because of global labour mobility. People just don't move away from their home country anymore. There is a continuous back and forth cycle.

We all know this century will be dominated by an Asian flavour. The sheer scale of China's growth is only matched by our doubts and fears. That's one of the reasons why Mandarin classes are probably not available at your local high school.

Your children will have a great advantage if they learn an Asian language, practice thinking interculturally, and become at ease in this increasingly global age.

So, you're probably glad nearly 70,000 international students came to BC last year. You're probably imagining how great it is for that student from Penticton to be paired up with that student from Shanghai.

The truth may surprise you.

Many teachers, educational institutions, and communities still find it hard to get around to a very simple notion: the experience with international students is not about what they can get from us.

The arrival of these guests is a gift, and it is mainly spurned. Many international students come to this country only to be stuck in a classroom with other international students. Few make long and abiding friendships with Canadians.

Canada is one of the greatest multicultural experiments in the world. People from all over the world have graced us with their talents. But something is wrong. We want the talent, investment, and restaurants, but many of us don't want to be altered.

When the Irish, Scottish, Germans, Russians, Italians, and Brits came here, they did something some have nearly forgotten: they assimilated and lost much of their own original cultures.

Many things are lost when you assimilate. You often forget that you were once a stranger.

This is why I, too, am part of this problem. Deep in my heart, I know I am suspicious of difference. Difference scares me. It brings fear and suspicion.

Understanding, embracing, and becoming comfortable with difference may be the Project of the Century for our classrooms, kitchens, churches, and streets.

But how is it to be done? Perhaps we can start by asking ourselves what kind of world we want for our children and grandchildren. Do we want them to perpetuate the fear of the stranger or do we want them to break the cycle, to disrupt the fear?

Where do you stand? Intercultural learning asks us to develop the ability to see that our values and beliefs are shaped by culture not by innate superiority. The dominant culture is not the best culture; it just happens to be the more powerful one.

There are many ways to cook, many ways to dress, and many ways to worship. There are many ways to think about clouds, rivers, and animals. There are many ways to act, behave, and adapt even as you retain your own values.

Cultural intelligence may be one of the new competencies that we must teach in our schools in order to prepare this new and better world. Cultural intelligence, like emotional intelligence, begins with empathy. It begins with recognizing yourself in the Other. Everyone feels. Everyone hurts. We are all lost. By learning to adapt, be flexible, enact tolerance, we prepare ourselves, not only for the Asian century, but for the Indigenous one.

Indigenous knowledge, unlike European modes of knowledge that dominate the west, teach us different things and possess an important critique of the ideas we hold dear.

Indigenous ideas about progress, competition, the natural world, even about our spiritual connection with this planet; these ideas are extremely valuable as they fuel new discoveries in medicine and social science.

But it is our deepening relationship with First Nations, Metis, and Inuit people of Canada that may be the greatest gift we can offer to new Canadians.

Let us, if we can, open our hearts to the gifts of our visitors, as we were once visitors, too. Let us start, if we are brave enough, with acknowledging our troubled, ambivalent, and potentially transformational connection with our first peoples.

Let our fear of the stranger be transformed.

The Silence
of the
Long Distant Lover

The poplars shiver outside the kitchen window. We are putting away groceries. The rhythm of daily life. How do I understand your silence? I slide the box of linguini next to the box of lasagna. Where does this go again?

The timbre of your silence. The long tone. The low volume of your non-verbal. You put away the grapes, mushrooms, and onions. The fridge beeps, "you left me open." What is this silence between us? We are the pop, scratch, and click before the music plays. This is the place we go – before we go.

Anywhere.

The spaghetti pot rests beside the sink. I am waiting to put it away. What are you saying with your lips sealed? What do you hear between the domesticities of words? Upstairs and downstairs and all over this house, your body speaks in a curved language.

There is a universe between us that I am trying to love.

Downstairs you work at the laundry of your silence. The cycles of permanent press. The to and fro of what we do not say. Upstairs, I wash the inside of the cast iron frying pan. The insides do not stick to the darkness.

201

It was years ago, near Maryfield, Saskatchewan. A dark Sunday night on our way home in December. Father is driving. I am pretending to drive because I am six years old. We listen to windshield wipers missing the dry snow. Looks like hyper drive.

What do you hear?

Time, time, time. The rolling seasons of love. The gaps in our conversations remind me of gaps in our other conversations.

My mother and father lived and loved for a long time. How long can we rotate these same gestures? How long can we play one note?

Silence is not mute. It is not non-being. It is a vibration of you with me, the walls of separation rubbing. Like this soapy cast iron pan, the part of me that doesn't stick to you is silent.

Our unbelonging drives the friction of our lovemaking. How do we love deeply when we do not understand each other's silence?

The eggs go to the left. The butter on the right. My silence is sometimes nothing. It is sometimes everything. At night, in the TV room below, the moon pulls on our discontent. Do the children feel the gravity of our lightness?

The silence insists on escaping. Giddy up, you say.

Hold me with your silence. Your tongue fills my mouth. There is no sound to how we dissolve at the edges of our edges. What is you? What is me?

You say, hold me and tightly let me go.

I know the part of you that is tired of me is quiet, like the washing machine at night. Waiting patiently to be opened, to let the energy escape, to infiltrate the spaces between the canned tomatoes, our Toyota, and the neighbour's unspent logs.

Energy is silence. A leaf unrolling. In your heart. The opening

Gretel

in Whistler

"Am I alone? Spies
hiss in the stillness, Hansel,
we are there still and it is real, real,
that black forest and the fire in earnest."
Louise Gluck

Before she rolls out of her bed in the morning, my sister lies still
and checks for pain. Her rheumatoid arthritis can be disabling, but
she has kept the autoimmune disease at bay through exercise and
lifestyle. It's hard to know exactly what she means by lifestyle.

She walks downstairs to her piano studio where she has made
a small bed for me. I've slept nearly ten hours which is a lot more
than I usually get, but I can barely get up to check my work phone
for messages.

"You ready?" she asks.

"Okay."

I don't know if I'm ready to go for a long walk. Visiting my
sister is like going on vacation and the first thing that always hits
me is how tired I am. From her basement window, I can see snow-
covered peaks and the circular shape of a cirque.

"How" long are you going to be?" she asks.

"Three minutes," I say quickly.

My sister lives in Whistler, a ski resort two hours north of Vancouver. She has lived there most of her adult life with her husband, two teenage boys, and doodle dog who refuses to come to me. Like most people, she considers her life pretty average, despite a 60 student piano studio and a design consulting business on the side.

Hardly average, I say to myself.

We jump into her station wagon with heated steering wheel and leather upholstery. We drive to a little known area away from the Olympic tourists. There are remnants of old cabins and an old mill from the days when Whistler was a yet undeveloped fishing camp. We meet up with her friend Heather, who holds a golden retriever and a cup of coffee. There are little plastic bags tied like flowers to the dog leash.

"Where do you live?" she asks.

I tell her and we are off on a fast-paced walk on the valley trail, an iconic series of trails that my sister helped design when she worked as a landscape architect and planner for the resort municipality.

Look at the sky, she exclaims. Heather looks great for 50. She skis, looks after her teens, plays squash, and seems to be the kind of stunning practical woman my sister has become.

I didn't know what to say to women without careers before, my sister said on the way to Heather's gorgeous lakeside place.

My sister explains it is a significant family achievement to position someone who can play the role of family caregiver without being forced into the workplace.

Although I know women who find being at home difficult and still others who seem to mainly shop and attend yoga classes, I don't say anything.

"I don't miss the regular job," says my sister who walks her dog every morning as if it were the most important thing a person could do. Maybe it is, I wonder.

"Look at that sky," says Heather again. We might have to head up and gets some runs in. What a life, I say to myself. If I had this kind of time, what would get me up in the morning? Would I look as good as these two? Do I even like myself enough to care for myself in this way?

The walk feels so good.

It is February and the skies have cleared. Even though the 2010 Olympics are on with the women's downhill being held on the mountain today, the locals know where to ski and find solace even under the noses of 50,000 visitors.

I can barely keep pace with the women and their dogs. They chat amiably, but they are moving fast. They point out changes in the landscape. The village is now investing in public art. There is a new train station on Nita Lake. Heather's husband is a custom builder. My sister's husband is a city manager.

My sister is about 5'4". She is three inches taller than our mother. She is the type of woman who communicates clearly with people. Some would call her direct.

When we were very young, our parents left us for a year in Korea while they went to Canada. We lived with our grandmother in Seoul. I remember the newspaper in the outhouse. My sister was about two years old. I was nearly four. There is a black and white photograph of me holding her hand. It is the Korean way to be told repeatedly to take care of your younger siblings.

I wonder now what I told her when our parents left. I wonder, too, what I told her when we met our parents again in Canada. We didn't recognize them. I even asked for proof, which made my mother cry. They were strangers to us.

We were Hansel and Gretel. To be abandoned and then adopted by strangers. She didn't talk for the longest time. Her only constant was me. My only constant was her. My sister and I are one.

When she was in Grade five, my sister sprained her ankle at the ski hill. She held up pretty well. She was carried onto the school bus where I waited for her. I hid because I didn't want her to know I was sobbing. I was supposed to take care of her, and I had failed.

I have grown up to be a caretaker kind of person, but I am now aware my sister has always considered this trait to be a bit of a weakness. Before I married, she told me she wanted me to find someone to protect me. I listened to this advice because before then I had no idea that my sister saw how foolish I really was.

"You're not like me," she says to me on the trail under the icy blue sky. "You don't know how not to care."

When you watch your sister grow up, you like to think that you're partially responsible for your sister's successes. I grew up trying to entertain her, make her giggle, and get her to act more like a brother.

I tried to teach her how to box, how to fish, how to wrestle, how to play tennis, and when we were older how to allow me to chase her female friends. She put up with her older brother's cavalier interests. She put up with me trying to pretend I had rescued her.

One of the biggest moments of my life was when my sister's husband left her. She doesn't know I constantly worried he wouldn't come back. I really missed him, but I knew it wasn't up to me to figure out how to save a young marriage.

It took my sister months of therapy and soul-searching to travel across the country to Nova Scotia to get her husband back – to feel what it is to apologize from the deepest part of you – and to know what it means to rescue love from heartbreak.

Only that little girl in the photograph would know.

I'm not the smartest guy in the world when it comes to love, marriage, and relationships, but my kid sister taught me a lesson when she told me nearly seventeen years ago that her husband was coming back home. She told me they were going to build a family from a foundation of rescued love, Gretel's love that was to be forged from mistakes and humility and forgiveness.

When I go to Whistler, I am treated to an insider's view of the spectacular jewel that has admirably hosted the 2010 Olympics. But most of all I am treated to the company of my sister and brother-in-law who continually teach me not to fear the fire and the black forest.

The

Prairies

I will always love the prairies. They are a part of my existence, as much as any other place I have ever lived. The sky is huge. And although the land seems uniform, it is not. I remember days and days of walking through damp fields, finding purple crocuses hidden in ice crystals. I remember exploring small groves of trees filled with small birds, or lying on the green grass in our backyard and staring at the clouds moving across the sky.

I remember thunderstorms with lightning arcing across the sky. Hail like diamonds on dark bright days falling slowly, spiraling in the wind, and you running with your arms outstretched trying to land one on your tongue.

The prairies were also about my growing awareness of father's profession. He made it an objective to visit everyone in the congregation. The folks in town were the easiest, of course, and often he would go alone. He would sit there with the seniors, doing his best to small talk in his halting English with retired farmers, ex-seed salesmen, and white-haired women who wanted to tell him about their lives.

But on weekends, we would get into the car and travel to people's homes for dinner. These were invitations mainly, and sometimes they were not. Sometimes my father would invite himself over. And he would be warned. But we would go anyway. And in this way, he was fearless. In each person he met, he worked hard to try and find out what was important, what mattered most.

We walked through many a farm. My mother saw many an outhouse that brought her memories of the war and growing up in Manchuria. We saw cattle, pigs, and chicken. We were shown dead coyotes, dead chicken, and dead foxes, all with their heads dangling and eyes still.

My father shared, over weak tea or strong coffee and dry biscuits, his life in Korea; wringing chickens with his hands, trudging through ginseng fields with his platoon. We followed these farmers around, sidestepping the manure, as they proudly showed us their way of life.

Many of the people we visited were poor. So poor that after dinner we left their homes hungry, and we had to eat at home. Once I complained of it, and I was told never to speak like that again.

We ate venison a lot. My mother hated the smell, especially when fried, but she, along with my sister and I, smothered it with Heinz and held on. My father ate everything placed in front of him. We ate prairie chicken and unknown white fish. We went to the barn, and they would slaughter the meat for us, letting us know how important a visit from the minister and his family was to them.

Other times, we would visit and we would be turned away at the door. Something was wrong. Sometimes it was a wife crying with cheeks red from sobbing or slapping. Sometimes it was a health problem, a farmer who had had a heart attack or a stroke. During these times my mother was instructed to cook her best bulgogi, Korean barbecue beef, and bring it to the tiny hospital. She served it with sticky rice in white CorningWare.

Sometimes the farms we visited were so far away we would

return well after midnight, the headlights showcasing the array of night insects, the windshield layered with smashed carcasses of moths and grasshoppers. My father would carry us in and lay us down on our beds and smooth the hair from our foreheads.

The hardest part for us was sitting at the dinner table trying to decide what to do. It seemed every family had its own customs. Some waited to pray. Others possessed little table manners. Others expected my father to come up with grace, and we would all bow our heads, and me, because it was my own father, would look around at everyone to see if they were peeking. Most of the time, the only person peeking was me, and sometimes, although he tried not to show it, my own father.

In the winter, when the snow was well over our heads, we'd find our driveway already shoveled. Sometimes it was a teenager who grew to love my father for his attention to his issues, his pregnant girlfriend, his abusive father, his need to escape to the nearest city. Sometimes it was a seventy-year-old man, still mourning his wife, who came in the early dawn with his gloves, toque, and tractor. I wanted to run out and thank him, but my father said no, Son, that man doesn't even come to church. Sometimes my father conducted weddings and received hugs and kisses and $50 tips. Sometimes he met people at funerals and they mowed our lawn or left green beans or corn for us on our doorstep.

At Christmas we received gifts that surprised us. Many of the poorest people brought us 25 pound turkeys that my mother would let languish in the basement freezer. She did that because, frankly, in Korea, there are no turkeys, and she didn't know how to cook them. Others brought us baked pies, or socks knitted under the light of a wood stove. My sister and I received attention, too. I received a hockey stick and a cowboy hat. My sister got a plastic flute and a doll. We never understood Christmas until we moved to Saskatchewan.

In the early 70s, being a minister in a small community was an important job. The church was an important place. It, aside from the hockey and curling rink, was the centre of life. Canada felt young. It felt new. It felt on the verge of something wonderful.

In our classes we sang "God Save the Queen" and belted out "Oh, Canada." We also squished under our desks in a feeble attempt to prepare for nuclear war. Sometimes I stared out the classroom window wondering if I would see blossoming Russian parachutes. And then I wondered what the Russians would possibly want with the prairies. Did they want the flat land and the dry lakes? How would they handle the people who seemed so plain, so resolute, and so good?

The television flickered nightly. Our family gathered to watch Walt Disney and the Walton's on Sunday nights. Somehow we knew in those early years in Saskatchewan that every family was doing what we were doing. They ate their dinners in front of Hockey Night in Canada on Saturday nights. And on Sunday mornings, they would go to church. And on Sunday evenings the kids would take a shallow hot bath, brush their teeth, and say their prayers before sleep.

For us it was no different. We were becoming Canadians. My father bought curling boots and tried throw a rock to the button. My mother tried making scalloped potatoes, and once in a while, she would thaw out a turkey and put it in the oven.

Statistical

Sweet Nothings

We all have a long list of regrets. I regret every mishap, especially car accidents and snowboard crashes where I land on my head and forget things afterward. I regret other things, too: humiliations, embarrassments, and mistakes that play in my head like a pop song from the 80s.

I've made many mistakes with people. As you get older, you try harder to be wise, purposeful, and courageous in all that you do. Courageous, not just in the physical sense, but in the sense that we learn to face the things that frighten us.

In the past I have been a coward about many things, skulking out of the room instead of raising my voice. Emotional and intellectual courage is the challenge of a lifetime. It takes guts to face and acknowledge that which triggers your deepest fears.

All of us, for example, find it difficult to face personal criticism. Even the strongest must learn to recognize the statistically valid fact that not everyone will agree with us, like us, or respect our point of view.

Being misunderstood is part of life, but accepting that fact isn't the journey of life; nor is the movement from cowardice to courage the journey either. My real problems lie outside my own awareness.

It's no wonder we can feel smug as we grow older. We believe that we are indeed facing down our perceived obstacles that, yawn, our fears are gradually becoming like comfortable shoes. We are used to being how we are, we accept our nature, and we decide, sooner or later, not to care about that which we do not care about (or even know about).

But perhaps what we don't know about ourselves IS the undiscovered country. After all, often what we do not know informs the opinions of others. You may not know exactly how you may come off to another (and may not care) but that person's view of you should not be ignored. Not because you should accept another's perceptions and judgments, but because you should at least attempt to understand what occurs outside your own awareness and measure this against your own sense of yourself.

Do you know what people really think of you?

You think you know your strengths and weaknesses, but how do you really know? Like all those really bad singers on American Idol, you might be fooling yourself. For example, you might think you're a really great friend, but your friends might not actually think so. You might think you're generous; others may say that you're always looking for an advantage in your generosity. You may wonder why you don't get invited to many parties; others may say you're competitive, hiding your insecurity. You may think you're a wonderfully curious columnist with a lot on his mind; others may say you've an irritating propensity for introspection as well as bad breath.

I have often thought of myself as the *smart guy* or the *creative guy*. But some of my friends disagree. They say I am the *controlling guy*. I'm the guy who always wants to drive the bus. How much truth is there in the perception of others? We all know someone who considers themselves the honest guy; the one who has the guts to tell it like it is. Well, we all want to tell this person, give it a rest, your famous bluntness is not making you very much fun to work with.

At parties, we all know people who squeal "I'm a people person," but after you meet them you feel like running for the chip dip. People believe all kinds of things about themselves without ever looking in the mirror of other people's perceptions.

So I have decided to interview my wife. Shouldn't your life partner be able to tell you the unseen truth about yourself?

Me: So, dear wife, how are you?

Her: Okay. You?

Me: I'm okay. Happy to be married, I'd say.

Her: Very funny. What do you want?

Me: I'm doing a column on self-deception.

Her: Right up your alley.

Me: So, can I ask you some questions about me?

Her: Shoot.

Me: Why do you love me?

Her: Huh?

Me: Come back here. Sit down. Please . . .

Her: You're asking me: Why do I love you?

Me: Yeah.

Her: Well, let me think, I guess it's because of the way you make me feel.

Me: What? You haven't mentioned my soaring intelligence, heightened creativity, unbelievable leadership skills, or the A I got in physical education 11.

Her: My dear husband, I love you because of the way you make me feel, not because of all your accomplishments, trips to

Ottawa, or high school reports cards.

Me: Let me get this straight. I asked you that question because I wanted to find out something about myself, but instead I find out, and pardon me if this sounds a bit harsh, that the facts of my existence, your judgment of who I am, is simply seen in the inescapable perspective of your own ego?

Her: So?

Me: I don't get it.

Her: Look, honey, instead of giving you some quasi-objective view of you as a jumble of historical, personal and biographical narratives or other ego-gratifying perspectives that I'm sure you'll eat up, I am simply stating the reason I love you is the way you make me feel.

Me: Really?

Her: Yeah.

Me: No way.

Her: Way.

Me: I don't get it.

Her: Dear husband, you are to me as I am to you. You would not like me let alone love me if I did not make you feel a certain way when we are together in the physical sense and beyond. In short, I need you to love me and most of the time I feel loved.

Me: But aren't my achievements important to you? Why am I putting all this effort in?

Her: Yes. I want to be loved by someone who I respect and admire.

Me: But couldn't you respect and admire anyone?

Her: True.

Me: Then I'm not really all that special in the romantic exceptional sense but more special in the statistically valid sense that we have enough in common for us to love each other.

Her: You like saying statistically, don't you? It kind of gets me hot.

Me: Am I mister right or mister right here and right now?

Her: Love isn't quite a lottery; it's more like a decision, a deep-seated decision.

Me: I really hate deep-seated decisions. They remind me of deep-seated pants and I am too young for them.

Her: If you say so.

Me: So here I am under this illusion about what makes me special to you and I find out that it's all about . . . commitment?

Her: It's more than that, because the commitment has be acted upon every day. Like when you'll vacuum the house later.

Me: Be serious.

Her: A commitment ONLY means something when you actually do something, whether consciously or not, to make me feel loved, every day.

Me: What?

Her: Sometimes you do stuff that I don't think you're aware of that I absolutely love. I love the way these actions make me feel.

Me: Really? So now, you're finally starting to answer the question: what do you love about me?

Her: Well, okay, if you want to put it that way, but isn't it the same with me? You say that you want to examine the impact of a person's presence outside that person's perceptions, right?

Me: Yeah.

Her: Well, I love the way you care about me, even when all it may mean that day is the way you love our children. I love the way you love others, me included. And how we talk during commercials.

Me: You love the kind of TV watcher I am?

Her: Sort of.

Me: And I love you how make me feel, too. I love how you embrace life.

Her: I love how you see the best in me.

Me: I guess that's why we're together.

Her: Anymore more questions?

Me: Nope. Walk with me.

Her: Where are we going? Hey, it's not Sunday morning, you know.

Me: I want to show you something deep-seated.

Her: Oh my.

Me: I'll whisper sweet statistical nothings in your ear.

Her: No way.

Me: Way.

A Visit from Grandmother

When I was in Grade five, my grandmother died. This was the mid-70s. She came to Canada in 1972, a small but stocky 60 year old woman who spoke little English. She stayed with us in Williams Lake for less than a year. Then she found a second story apartment overlooking Main Street in Vancouver.

The neon from the car dealer flashed into her apartment at night. It wasn't the greatest area, but she rode the electric buses, took care of herself, and waited for our visits. We were all very relieved she no longer lived with us.

At the age of 11, I believed I was the only one who could understand my grandmother. The anger boiled inside her, and it didn't take much for her to start pounding the floors and walls while using the most exotic of swear words. After these episodes, I would sit in my room, wondering if I should go to her, hold her hand, and listen to her. But I did not.

"Your father is useless," she would yell. "He's supposed to be a minister, but he can't even take care of his poor mother!"

Over the years, these memories, cloudy and confused, have made me dizzy. The four-year-old in me wants to believe she tried to separate me from my parents, and so I ended up eating her food and tormenting her. The revenge of a four-year-old. People say it is easy to forget, especially when you are young, but I wish I could remember better. The year I lived with her in Korea, after my parents had left for Canada, did something to me.

When she lived with us in Williams Lake, I treated her very poorly. I was older and felt there was nothing she could do to me. My father, mother, and sister were not only afraid of her, but we talked about her behind her back. We talked about how loudly she chewed her food. We made fun of her broken English. We greeted her old country cooking with mock horror.

I was probably the worst, because I feared her so little. I was rebellious, disrespectful, and spoiled. One day she made us some delicious soft white buns with sweet red beans inside. It took her two days to make them. I gobbled them up greedily without appreciation. I was horrible and nobody stopped me. Finally, she decided to live in Vancouver.

(Whenever anyone came to visit us, it didn't take long for us to drive that person away. Other than saying we were awful people; I do not know why. We tore people apart with petty criticisms and resentments.)

My grandmother grew up in a small peasant village on a volcanic island between Korea and Japan. She spent most of her life under Japanese occupation. Living under occupation, as most Koreans of that generation will tell you, strengthens your identity. But you pay the price because of the resentment that rots your stomach like acid. My grandmother, Bong Choon Chung was an illiterate single parent and a born-again Christian. She survived by growing vegetables and taking them to market on weekends. She was married twice. My grandfather died shortly after my father was born. The second man she married, left to work in Manchuria, not long after my uncle was born.

When we heard grandmother had died, we drove in our Mercedes down to Vancouver. It was a seven-hour drive that passes through many geo-climatic zones. We passed 100 Mile House, Clinton, Yale, Chilliwack, and finally arrived in Vancouver where the air was moist and faintly smelling of cedar and ocean.

She was buried in Vancouver on a cold day. The funeral service, the first for me, was attended by Korean families throughout the lower mainland. Today, there is a huge population of Koreans, but in those days, it seemed we all knew each other. The day after we arrived my father's half-brother, an electronics businessman from Chicago, burst into our hotel room and blustered promises to us.

"You kids. You study hard. I pay for your university. Your grandmother was murdered by bad doctor, and I make sure he pays. Tomorrow, we go shopping and I buy you anything you want."

Of course, none of these things happened. My grandmother died as a result of a gall bladder surgery complications, and my uncle didn't hire or know any hit men. I don't even know where my uncle is now. I hear he is keeping a low profile in the Pacific Northwest after he scammed a large retailer out of a cheque large enough to retire on.

Korean funerals are a little different. First of all, there is the custom of envelope giving. People lined up at the hotel room and slipped my father thick envelopes. Afterwards, I saw my father count up the stacks and stacks of cash, and to me, it seemed like a scene out of a Hollywood movie.

The next day, we sat in a long white limousine and arrived at the church. I sat in a hard pew beside my little sister. My parents entered behind the casket and that's when I heard the long low and nearly hysterical cries of my father. I had never heard that sound before and I've never heard it again. Then my mother joined in. Her cries filled the church and she collapsed. I hung my head, closed my eyes, and could not understand.

Seeing our mother cry, made my sister and I cry, too. I wondered if my grandmother was watching us. Our sadness, our sorrow, our guilt. There were so many things to cry for, but who really understood what it was like for my grandmother.

Later, we drove to the cemetery. I was amazed by the long row of cars behind us. To be the centre of attention in this way was strange. People who I didn't know, bowed to my parents and embraced them. I stood in the distance. Nobody shook my hand or clapped me on the shoulder. Finally, a relative stood beside me, and I felt better, at least someone recognized me.

On that cold November day, there were no tears for my grandmother. I blinked hard and tried, but the wind cooled my eyes, and I kept looking up for snow. A bit of frozen rain moved diagonally as people put up their black umbrellas. There were a lot of people there, but it was very quiet. The sleet hit the ground and bounced. For a moment, I could see snow on Grouse Mountain and then the cloud cover came. There was a lot of mud around the casket, but the ground was hard. I waited for my uncle to do something hysterical, but he stood with his hands in his pockets and kept pushing up his glasses.

My parents wiped their eyes.

We never visited my grandmother's grave except maybe once, the following year, and for some reason, all I can remember is my mother putting plastic flowers next to her bronze marker.

It has been many decades now and I have not visited my

grandmother. I know her grave sits at Ocean View Cemetery, and I try not to wonder about what kind of person I was and have become. After all, I am too busy. I am a father now with young children of my own. My own parents have passed on and left us alone.

It is April, and my daughter has just turned nine. Clementine still cries when I leave town on business. She misses me. I wonder how old she will be before she stops crying. How long will she love me like this? And what, I ask myself, when I sit in that hotel room far away, have I done to deserve those beautiful tears.

I think about tears. The tears in my daughter's eyes, the tears in my own, and the frozen tears in the sky the day my grandmother was buried. I think about how it must have been for me to lose my parents for that year while they settled in a new land. And how it must have been for my little sister who believed she'd never see her parents again. And how it must have been for my grandmother who stayed in Korea to raise us, and love us, and who is now nearly forgotten.

River

of Love

Your mother teaches you one simple thing above all others: how to love. Your mother shows you love, and you go out and practice, stumbling, fumbling, at once embracing and rejecting the river of her love. You love her and respect her, but you also think you know where the river ends.

The love that my mother showed me was at once beautiful and flawed. Her love is my map. It tells me where to go and where not to go. The current is steady with faithfulness, serenity, purpose, and obedience. Beneath the surface lies silence, suffering, anger, and bitterness. She cannot leap the banks and find a different way.

I did not know any of these things in November 1994 when I brought my mother to the guest room above the garage in my suburban home in Prince George, British Columbia.

In July I was married, and she came to the wedding yellow-faced, jaundiced. I ruined my honeymoon with distraction and worry. In September, she was finally diagnosed with pancreatic cancer. In October, her surgery was deemed a failure. In November, she was given a few weeks to live. Without hesitation, I brought her home.

We tended to her. We willed her to live. And she lived until June, a miraculous eight months. Together, we saw the seasons. We saw autumn leaves crumble, winter snows wash away, pussy willows pop, and we saw summer in full flight. I had her for the last eight months of her life. I cooked for her. I cleaned for her. I laughed with her, and I exercised with her. I lifted her in my arms and carried her to the toilet. I sang to her, injected her with morphine, and stroked her forehead. I served her as she had served me. Then I had to let her go.

In the end, I mothered my own mother, and I resisted losing her, even though it might have been better for her if I would have let her go sooner. But I could not. I could not let her go. And, in some ways, I still cannot.

Why? Because I know the truth about the entire experience of my mother's cancer, my care for her, and her death. Some called us noble. Some wondered how we survived the ordeal. Some asked how we did it. How did she live so long? How did she manage to walk until the very end when so many die in bed, only a shadow of their former selves? How did she manage to smile and care for others, as if she were supernatural?

I know the secret.

I know how she was able to pull it off. I even know how I was able to do the things I cannot believe I did. I know how it happened. I know how I got the strength and devotion. I know how she got the power. Yes, I know the secret. At every single moment of our eight months together, this frail Korean woman of 52, over-taken by a violent and fast-growing cancer, consumed with intense pain and agony, and still suffering from the loss of her husband to schizophrenia, was still mothering me.

I was her son. And she helped me through the whole thing. I was not mothering her. She was mothering me.

As I watched her die, as I watched her body shrink to 70 lbs, as I watched her cheeks hollow, skin yellow, and energy dissipate, I watched her watching me, thinking more of me than the cancerous state of her own body. I knew that mothering was not just a particular kind of love, not just a selfless and enduring love, and not just a role to be played by an actor. I did not know when I discovered my mother's body in our guest room, lifeless and still, the heat disappearing quickly, how long her love would last.

Is it in every good and dark thing I do?

Our mothers give us life. And death. And longing. And the deepest of our regrets.

And when your mother dies, you feel so sorry for yourself. You feel like crying and you do. And the wail is often a baby's wail. It is, in an adult man, a strange and beastly sound. I roared and I wondered, at the same time, exactly who was roaring.

My wife found me in the basement, lost in a much-needed nap.

"Your mother is gone," she said.

"What?" I said. "No, she can't be."

Then she grabbed me, pulled me down, and sat with me on the carpeted stair to the laundry room. She held me in her arms, as I sobbed and wondered who I was now . . . now that my mother was gone.

Was I the little boy who misses his mommy, the woman who eternally cheers him, forgives him, and worships him? Was I the adolescent boy who sees his mother as a nuisance, a nosy caregiver, an appendage of his father? Or was I the grown man who sees his mother as his best connection to the past and his best insight into the future?

In the days after her death, I began to fall back to earth. Hours would go by when I didn't think of her. A day would go by and would have forgotten to think of her. Now it's down to once every couple of days.

I think about my mother. Sometimes when I'm really sick I wish she could come to me in her flannel nightgown, put a cold compress on my forehead and sit on my bed. Sing me a song. Sometimes, for no reason, when I see something beautiful, like the sun, the sky, a mountain, or my daughter's eyes. I want to cry. I want to sob. I feel so sorry for myself. I want to mourn her.

But I am a man without a mother now. I am a man who has lost his mother. I am a man who must go on without his mother's love. So I hold my son and daughter now. I hold them tightly. I hold them secretly when they don't know it. When I hug them goodbye in the morning when they leave for school, I hold them tightly, and I don't want to let them go. I want to fix time, so they do not grow. I want to fix time, so love cannot change. I want to fix time, so we do not die.

Sometimes I imagine she's watching. But I know my mother is gone, that she does not exist, that I cannot step into the same spot in the river twice. She does not exist. That's what I say. That's what I write. Pages in my hand. Pages in my hand.

I am afraid to scatter the ashes that sit in the yellow cedar box. She is not scattered. If I let her go, where will I be? The river of love is flowing, calling me to the ocean, where it is warm and salty and crimson, where I can go to sleep and dream of her no more.

Listening

to Listening

I hear you. I hold your eyes in my ears. I feed deep upon what you say. But more importantly I discover what you don't say. The things you don't say. The absences. The hollows of your body. What your mouth does when you look me.

What you don't say speaks to me.

When I listen to myself listening what do I hear? I hear the murmur of the seasons. The reverberation of our togetherness. The places where we have grown. The places where we are still sitting still. The places we are going.

The vast universe of possibility. The possibly of our co-evolving.

I am listening to my listening. What do I hear? I have recorded my listening. And when I playback my performance, I hear things that I have never heard before.

I hear my hot eagerness to respond. My throat overwhelms my ears. I rush to fill in the silence with argument, with rhetoric, with words that don't matter.

What is the sound of listening?

When I listen to my own listening, I hear new things. I hear your listening. The soft intent. Your beautiful openness. The open throat and the naked ear.

Your listening astounds me.

My own listening falls short, I realize. I cannot help the

competitive impulse. (I can barely control the need to control.) I fall helplessly into my own distracted silence. Not the open silence, but the closed silence of preoccupation.

I am not listening when I prepare what to say.

How difficult it is, to listen to one's own listening, to hear yourself stuttering and fumbling for the right words, when you know there are better ways for the body to express itself.

And there are times, too, when we are both listening, when our hearts beat together, and we embrace in a way that speaks of our mutual appreciation.

When a child is delighted by the teacher's humility. When grace is measured and noted. When we know and feel, when we are there together sharing two versions of a reality that is beautifully ambiguous.

I love how you make me feel. Especially when we don't hear the same things and still know we can be together. When our oneness is marked by an exquisite combination of two different people sharing a oneness.

There are times when I listen to you, and I hear new things that my heart cannot help but brim over with a sense of your uniqueness. And now, when I listen to how I listened, I also hear new things such as how delicate we are together. Such as how knowing we are of our sensitivities. How good we can be (about letting go) without saying we don't care.

Sometimes it's okay not to care. Doing nothing about something is an odd way of caring, but that's sometimes the best way to accomplish a thing. In another moment, we will see another slice of reality, we will find a new way discovering something new, and that glimpse will not only change how we see things now, but it will shape what is to follow.

When I listen to myself listen, I can see that listening changes things. That listening to listening changes things. That every moment is a chance to hear, hear again, and make the future different.

There is no one past. Every time we listen to our listening, we create another version of the way things were and the way things are going to be.

I am becoming new when I listen to myself.

Over and over again I hear what I've said and how I wish I could have said it better or heard it more accurately. In the last playback, things and lives are changed.

I look at your eyes. I see the soft pink of your lips. I hear the voices of our ancestors and the rustling of the wind.

I play your song again and again, and I feel the universe forming. I feel the alignment of particles, planets, and bodies. Your body whispers to me. Your body designs (me) to listen and re-listen and guides this force we call love.

I love listening to you. I love changing my knowledge by listening again and again. I feed deep upon your tears and my tears. I hear you blink, and breathe, and reach out for me in the darkness.

There you are. Again and again. Let me listen to your heart beat against mine.

Acknowledgements

This book celebrates ten years of the "Global Citizen," a bi-weekly column published in the Okanagan Sunday newspaper. I am very grateful for the faithful and steadfast readers of this Sunday morning column. Your encouragement makes this book possible.

I wish to thank the Kelowna Daily Courier, its publisher, and the great people who have edited my work. Thank you Tom Wilson for originating the column. Thank you Jon Manchester for shaping and strengthening its middle years. Thank you to editors David Trifunov and Doyle Potenteau, and to city editor Pat Bulmer, for supporting the column. Thank you Terry Armstrong, publisher of the Kelowna Daily Courier, for your stalwart support and enthusiasm.

It takes many relationships to keep a writer afloat. I moved several times during the last ten years and friends in Prince George, Kelowna, Victoria, Winnipeg, and Cranbrook allowed me to keep going especially when times were tough.

Debbie and Dave Paulson. Beryl and Albert Baldeo. Sue and Richard Chung. Keith Shanks and Krista Vejvan. Robin and Luis Calao. Ann McKinnon and Peter Urmetzer. Jill and Henry Kim. Jeanette and Rob Crobar. Anita Boehm and Siebe Kamstra. David Wong and Sue Ann Wong Yang. Dawn Robson and George Davison. Heidi and Bob MacPherson. Thank you for your early and consistent support.

Many colleagues also helped form this book including faculty and staff at College of New Caledonia, Okanagan College,

Camosun College, University of British Columbia, Red River College, University of Manitoba, Memorial University, and Thompson Rivers University.

Thank you Bob Belton, Peter Arthur, Kelly Pitman, Sonja Knutson, Virginie Magnat, Niigaan Sinclair, Louis Gordon, Eric Sehn, Michael Farris, Mare Fulber, Sybil Harrison, Kyra Garson, Joan Yates, Camille Callison, Judy Caldwell, Geoff Wilmshurst, Avery Hulbert, Dominic Bergeron, Kelly Doyle, Veronica Gaylie, Julie Vaudrin-Charette, Michael Minions, Anne-Marie Holmwood, Jeff Cooper, Robert Campbell, Dianne Teslak, Cathi Shaw, Jake Kennedy, Pat Bowron, Sean Johnson, and Sarah Loewen.

A writer needs mentors as well as friends and family. Thank you, Alex Dulic, Pauline Oliveros, Richard Atleo, Robert MacDonald, and Wayson Choy.

It is my dear loyal readers who I owe nearly everything. Thank you for staying with me Wong Wing Sui, Benny Min, Ana Lopez, Michelle Rule, Loren Lovegreen, Sterling Haynes, Carrie Ivardi, Cy Longman, Barbara Bailey, Jack Moes, Steve Robinson, Marilyn Raymond, Sherrin Western, Suzanne Johnson, Greg Krasichynsky, Wilda Schab, Lisa Ordell, Kathy Chin, Ellie Archer, Ash Andersen, Paul Varga, Brent MacDonald, Andy Gibbs, Susan Borowski, Donna Duke, Jeff Hopkins, Barry Milner, Cherie Hanson, Brenda Feist, Amy Grant, Deanna and Roland Kemperman, Greg Crawford, Brian Gebhardt, Emily Mayne, Phil Ashman, Tracey Dyer, Robert Buisson, Brenda Herrin, Dayna Anderson, Theresa Linnette, Sylvia Gibbs, Hazel MacClement, Patricia Leigh, Pauline Bennison, Nadine Naughton, Chris Brahar, Shawn Serfas, Viveka Johnson, Laurie Blackwell, David Kim, Marilyn Biletski, Christopher Horsethief, Marie Weale, Hong Ngueyen, Jamie

Vandenbossche, Darcy Nybo, Laura Cooper, Dawn Boudreau, Bessie Chow, Carol Cosco, Lin Hua, Lindy Munk, Codi Morigeau, Joanne Parker Robertson, Lise Gunby, Karen MacDonald, Keely Richmond, Jude Shirley, Brian Coombs, Melissa Hart, Robert Campbell, Johanna van Zanten, Jesse Nicholas, Beth Veenkamp, Daryl Eyjolfson, David Kuefler, Dale Mosher, Seanna Dombrosky, Frank Trenouth, Dorothy Tinning, David Walls, John Lent, Jim Taylor, Darren Handschuh, Ross Freake, Francie Greenslade, and Naheed Nenshi. I hope I remembered all of you.

I'd also like to thank my book editor and publisher, Darcy Nybo. Thank you for your dedication and professionalism.

Without my family, I would be nothing. Thank you to my children, Beckett and Clementine. I have learned so much from loving you.

I acknowledge that this book was compiled and edited on Ktunaxa land. Thank you, Ktunaxa people, for allowing me to exist here and be included in a small way on your journey.

About the Author

Sae Hoon Stan Chung is an award winning writer and much loved columnist. He was born in Seoul, Korea and raised in Canada. He has written, and spoken widely, in both public and academic forums.

He completed his PhD at the University of British Columbia, and wrote his dissertation on improvisation, performance, and the work of Pauline Oliveros. He is currently Vice President Academic and Applied Research at the College of the Rockies.

Stan is married with two children. He spends his time between West Kelowna and Cranbrook, BC.